Leckie×Leckie

HIGHER
French

grade **booster**

✕ Colin Hamilton ✕

ISBN 978-1-84372-709-5

Published by
Leckie & Leckie Ltd, 3rd floor, 4 Queen Street, Edinburgh, EH2 1JE
Tel: 0131 220 6831 Fax: 0131 225 9987
enquiries@leckieandleckie.co.uk   www.leckieandleckie.co.uk

Special thanks to
Aptara Inc. (design and page make up), Roda Morrison (copy-editing), Caleb Rutherford (cover-design), Jennifer Shaw (proofreading), Lisa G. Albarracin (content review).

A CIP Catalogue record for this book is available from the British Library.

® Leckie & Leckie is a registered trademark
Leckie & Leckie Ltd is a division of Huveaux plc.

Leckie & Leckie makes every effort to ensure that all paper used in our books is made from wood pulp obtained from well-managed forests, controlled sources and recycled wood or fibre.

Acknowledgements
We would like to thank the following for permission to reproduce their material:
SQA for permission to reproduce past examination questions (answers do not emanate from the SQA).

CONTENTS

1 Oral Assessment (Speaking)

Part 1: General

Part 2: Getting the grades

Part 3: Exemplary materials

PART 1: GENERAL

The relative importance of the oral assessment as part of the overall examination

The oral assessment – or speaking test, as you may call it in your school – is worth 25% of the overall marks of your external examination. It is also the part of your Higher French exam which you can prepare for the best, since you choose the actual topics for it and, as far as possible, prepare the language you are going to use. This has got to be a big motivator in itself! There is no doubt about it – if you are well enough prepared for your oral assessment, you should be getting a top grade for this part (one-quarter!) of your Higher French exam.

Oh, and another piece of good news – you need do only one speaking test in your entire French course, since the one oral assessment counts for both internal (or NAB) and external (or examination) assessments!

The advantages of sitting your oral assessment during a particular period

Another motivating factor is that schools can decide pretty much when they would like students to do the oral assessment. The majority of candidates sit their oral assessment at some point during the period mid-February to the end of March. The advantage of using this time to get part of a real Higher exam behind you is that it comes after the prelims and before the Easter holidays – in other words, a quarter of your exam in French will be secured well in advance of the formal examination schedule. *All* your subjects will be equally important of course, but at this particular period it makes sense to commit special time and effort to your French since the oral assessment actually counts towards 25% of the exam grade.

The actual oral assessment

Here are the basic facts you need to know about the oral assessment. It is divided into two parts:

- a **presentation** (of between 1½ and 2 minutes) on any topic from the course which is approved by your teacher, followed by
- a **discussion** (4½ – 6 minutes) where you are expected to answer questions, firstly relating to the presentation topic and then about a topic or topics from another of the three themes.

This is probably a good time to remind you of the themes and topics in the Higher French syllabus. It may well be that your school is following a textbook or perhaps many different materials, but your teacher(s) will certainly have made sure that you will eventually be covering the whole of the list below, possibly by combining some of the topics. However, it is equally likely that you will not have had time to study the entire list *yet* – don't forget you are sitting the oral assessment in either February or March, and study leave won't start until May! Don't panic. Just be careful to select those themes and topics which you consider to be your strengths.

 When choosing your presentation and discussion topics, you should dig out your old Credit or Intermediate notes, as these will help get you started.

Here is the list of the Higher French (Language Unit) Themes and Topics, as found in the SQA's most recent Arrangements Documents (9th edition, April 2007):

Themes	Topics	Topic development
Lifestyles	Family, friends, society	• issues in relationships with friends/family • role of the individual in the home and in society • advantages/disadvantages of home area
	Leisure and healthy living	• leisure interests • health issues
Education and work	School/college	• critique of own school/college • personal achievement to date such as in a record of achievement
	Careers	• job intentions and aspirations • employment issues

| Wider world | Holidays and travel | • comparison of types of holiday/travel
• past holidays/journeys |
| | Tourism | • critique of local area in Scotland as tourist centre
• areas of interest in target language country/countries and beyond |

The presentation topic/topic development will come from a particular theme, say lifestyles, and the discussion will start off with questions from your teacher relating in some way to that same area. However, it is very important to remember that the discussion will then move on to a *second* theme, say education and work, where you will have chosen *another* topic/topic development to discuss.

Planning for the oral assessment: a couple of examples

It may be helpful at this point to give a couple of examples of choices for the oral assessment that recent Higher French candidates have made.

Candidate A

Presentation: solo talk on 'les rapports domestiques chez moi' (from lifestyles theme).

Discussion: Part A: answer questions on: 'la liberté à la maison'; 'les travaux ménagers' (from lifestyles theme); then Part B: discuss 'le règlement au lycée'; 'la vie après le collège'; 'mes projets d'avenir' (from education and work theme).

Candidate B

Presentation: solo talk on 'la vie urbaine contre la vie campagnarde' (from lifestyles theme)

Discussion: Part A: answer questions on 'ce qu'il y a à faire dans ma ville'; 'comment rester en pleine forme' (from lifestyles theme); then Part B: discuss 'manger en Ecosse et en France – les différences culinaires' (from lifestyles theme); 'passer les vacances à l'étranger'; 'les vacances découverte' (from wider world theme).

Both candidates start off with their presentation based on the lifestyles theme, although they choose different topics. Both begin their discussion with questions which follow on from the presentation topic yet cover different areas of their first theme; the final part of the discussion sees candidates A and B answer questions from a second theme, education and work and wider world, respectively.

PART 2: GETTING THE GRADES

How to plan for the oral assessment

You have every chance of achieving a top grade in this part of the examination because it rewards candidates who can prepare thoroughly and commit a significant amount of what they have learned to memory. Of course, you will need to plan it properly, ensure the quality of language is your best, draft and re-draft according to your teacher's comments, and then rehearse your presentation and practise your discussion until you feel you are ready to perform at your best. You might find this type of systematic approach useful:

- Show your teacher a draft of the presentation, showing how it proceeds step-by-step.

 Remember that the best presentation titles or topics are those which are specific enough to allow you to go into some depth, yet general enough to encourage links with other subjects and to lead to a broad discussion later.

- As soon as you start writing out what you wish to say in this and future stages of the oral assessment, it is essential that you observe the rules of what makes quality language in Higher French. (This is discussed in full below: **How to achieve quality language**, page 12.)
- Once the rough draft is approved, make sure that you submit a full, written account of your presentation to your teacher, and take on board any comments and suggestions made before writing out the corrected version.
- You are now ready to learn this off by heart. As you probably have done on numerous occasions in your French career to date, divide the presentation up into small, manageable sections and begin to commit to memory. It will definitely help later on when you revise for the actual oral assessment that you have already learned it.

 Once you feel you know your stuff, enlist a friend or member of the family to listen to you, as this encourages you to see the oral assessment as a whole as a *performance.* Never mind what they think of you at home!

- Draft out how you might expect the first part of the discussion (which follows on from your presentation topic) to go.

Sketch out a mind map of areas which your teacher could reasonably refer to or questions he/she might ask in connection with the presentation.

- Write out a series of mini paragraphs, covering all the logical sub-topics. A good idea is to prepare for about 3 minutes' worth of discussion material. One advantage of this mini paragraphs approach is that it lends itself well to piece-by-piece learning off by heart later.

- Consider how you would like to link a topic from another theme to your first: what would follow on best from what you have just discussed? Check with your teacher that this would be a sensible topic to progress to from the previous one.

- Repeat the processes of the earlier discussion, producing eventually a series of mini paragraphs based on what you could reasonably expect from the teacher.

Think *laterally* as well as *logically:* if the teacher chose to go off on a tangent rather than follow the obvious route of discussion, what might he/she ask you about? What are some of the other potential areas of discussion that might come about? Be prepared for the unprepared!

- The best discussions often come from candidates who are prepared to take on another big topic of conversation, rather than just be content with the minimum. This is your opportunity to offer something special, to stand out as an excellent candidate, rather than just a satisfactory one. Verify with your teacher that this final topic would be acceptable.

- Repeat the earlier processes of drafting out the logical and the not-so-logical route of discussion, then writing out your mini paragraphs, before committing to memory step by step.

- You are now ready to refer to the checklist (page 13) to ensure that quality language is a central feature of your oral assessment. This checklist needs to apply to all aspects of your Higher French examination where you yourself produce the language – the oral assessment, the directed writing and the short essay after the listening. That is why this process of planning and learning is so important!

- Ideally, you should be able to organise a trial run or practice oral assessment with your teacher before the real thing. Apart from allowing you a complete dress rehearsal of the actual oral assessment, this practice session should enable your teacher to mark your performance by using the SQA's pegged marks system, which offers easily understood criteria to you, the candidate, and the teacher or marker. The SQA National Qualifications in Modern Languages document on the Assessment of Speaking at Higher clearly shows how you will be marked, and basically emphasises the importance of

  – *accuracy*

  – *fluency*

  – *extended responses*

  – *a wide range of vocabulary and grammar.*

So, to summarise:

1. Presentation
   - draft to teacher
   - 'quality language' check
   - learn by heart
   - practise with a good listener!

2. Discussion
   - draft to teacher
   - 'quality language' check
   - 2 distinct but linked topics, subdivided into...
   - mini paragraphs
   - learn by heart
   - practise with a good listener!

Finally...

- essential to go through at least one trial run before the actual test.

Categories	Criteria	Pegged marks	Pegged marks
		Presentation	Discussion
Very Good	Confident handling of language with a high level of accuracy.	10	15
	Speaks fluently and without undue hesitation, or where there is some hesitation recovers well, and readily goes beyond minimal responses.		
	Wide range of vocabulary and structures appropriate to Higher.		
	Immediate and almost total understanding of almost everything said.		
	Pronunciation and intonation sufficient to be readily understood by a speaker of the language.		
Good	The language is mostly accurate, with a wide range of language and structures appropriate to this level.	8	12
	Speaks fluently and without undue hesitation, or where there is some hesitation recovers well, and generally goes beyond minimal responses.		
	Understands almost everything said. Pronunciation and intonation sufficient to be understood by a speaker of the language.		
Satisfactory	Completes task, demonstrating sufficient accuracy in a range of language and structures appropriate to this level, to convey meaning clearly, in spite of errors.	6	9
	May be hesitant and give only minimal correct responses or speak at greater length with less accuracy.		
	Capable of coming to an understanding of all that is said.		
	Pronunciation and intonation sufficient to be understood by a sympathetic speaker of the language.		

continue on next page

Categories	Criteria	Pegged marks	Pegged marks
		Presentation	Discussion
Unsatisfactory (Near Miss)	Difficulty in achieving communication because of limited range of vocabulary and structures and/or serious inaccuracies in language appropriate to Higher.	4	6
	Understands most of what is said clearly and slowly by a sympathetic speaker.		
	May speak with a considerable degree of hesitation, but makes some attempt to recover.		
	Pronunciation and intonation sufficient to be generally understood by a sympathetic speaker of the language.		
Poor	Communication seriously impeded by inadequate vocabulary and structures and/or by gross errors in language appropriate to Higher.	2	3
	Frequently has difficulty in under-standing what is said, even with help.		
	There may be occasional other tongue interference.		
	Pronunciation and intonation may be such as to require clarification, even from a sympathetic speaker of the language.		
Very Poor	No redeeming features.	0	0

We find in the Arrangements Documents (last published in 2007), where details are given of a Grade C (equivalent to *Satisfactory*) and a Grade A (equivalent to *very good*).

 It is worth remembering that you can still get an overall Grade A in your French Higher even if you only manage a Grade C in one element!

Grade C	Grade A
Makes a short, prepared presentation on a chosen topic, and sustains discussion in a manner comprehensible to a sympathetic speaker of the target language.	Makes a short, prepared presentation on a chosen topic, and sustains discussion easily. Expands on ideas and opinions expressed in the presentation.
Content	**Content**
• Goes beyond exchange of factual/social information to express points of view. • Organises content of presentation to have clear start and conclusion. • Sustains discussion by going at times beyond minimal responses.	• Expresses ideas and opinions clearly and acknowledges different points of view. • Organises content of presentation to have clear start, progression of ideas and conclusion. • Sustains discussion by offering additional information/comments fairly frequently.
Understanding	**Understanding**
• Understands most of what is said directly to him/her when clearly articulated. • Repetition/reformulation may be required.	• Understands almost all of what is said directly to him/her when clearly articulated. • Asks for repetition and/or clarification as required.
Speaking	**Speaking**
• Accent, intonation and pronunciation are sufficient to ensure communication; shows some awareness of rules. • Shows sufficient control of the rules of grammar appropriate to this level to ensure communication in spite of errors. • Language characterised by mostly simple sentences and reliance on high-frequency verbs and other words.	• Shows good awareness of rules of intonation and pronunciation. • Shows good control of the rules of grammar appropriate to this level and makes few errors of a major nature. • Language characterised by some complexity of structure and range of vocabulary.

How to achieve 'quality' language

Now that you have considered your approach to planning for the oral assessment and have familiarised yourself with the SQA documents on what is expected of your performance, it is time to examine, in detail, how you can reach a top grade. In other words, what are the actual ingredients or features of your spoken French that make up a *very good* or *grade A* performance?

We can turn to lots of areas for help with this. Firstly, it is important to remember that what you learned for Standard Grade speaking tests remains good for Higher, too, and that you are *not* starting from scratch. The Grade Related Criteria, as they were interpreted by your teacher when you were in s4, are still relevant in terms of what is expected of you at Higher.

 Reusing and updating some of what you learned for your most successful Standard Grade speaking and writing assessments will involve some quality language at this level and can be a confidence booster!

Secondly, the SQA have published something called the Productive Grammar Grid in the Arrangements Documents (Appendix A) for all levels of French, from Intermediate 2 through to Advanced Higher, in order to show candidates and teachers what to aim for in the language you produce in speaking and writing. It is not an easy read, but it does underline the importance of *a high level of accuracy* and *a wide range of grammar and vocabulary*.

Thirdly, and most importantly, you should think carefully about those aspects of spoken (and written) French which receive special and frequent attention during your Higher course, because these are the characteristics which you must build into your oral assessment. Of course, I don't necessarily mean *all* of them. But you do have to cover a *convincing number of them*, and do so in such a way as to assure your teacher and the SQA that you *really know, and can apply, the rules of grammar and vocabulary*.

So, if I were to boil down the essential features of Grade A language in the oral assessment, my checklist would look something like this:

Quality language checklist

- **time phrases** (for past, present and future tenses – e.g. *L'année dernière; cette année; l'année prochaine,* etc.)

- **present tense** (regular and irregular verbs; two verbs together – e.g. *Je déteste faire…; je peux aller…,* etc.)

- **future tenses** (both *nous allons voyager* and *nous voyagerons* types)

- **perfect tense** (for single, completed actions in the past, with avoir and être verbs, regular and irregular verbs – e.g. *on a joué…; je suis allé(e)…; nous avons mangé…; ils ont bu…,* etc.)

- **imperfect tense** (for either repeated actions in the past or describing in the past – e.g. *j'allais tous les jours…; c'était magnifique…,* etc.)

- **modal verbs** (joining two verbs together to express intentions, hopes, possibilities, etc. – e.g. *Je voudrais étudier…; on pourrait visiter…,* etc.)

- **range of subjects/subject pronouns** (i.e. not just *je*; use of interesting subjects, – e.g. *les jeunes pensent que…; les professeurs sont…,* etc.)

- **adjectives and adverbs** (ensure your adjectives 'agree' with what they describe: *ma mère est très protectrice,* etc.; use adverbs to strengthen meaning: *je la trouve incroyablement énervante*)

- **various expressions of opinion** (full range of *à mon avis…; selon mes parents…,* etc.)

- **different ways of providing reasons and explanations,** to follow on from your opinions (*parce que…; puisque…; c'est-à-dire…,* etc.)

- **questions** (often posed to introduce a topic or issue, e.g. *Faut-il toujours obéir aux parents?* or *Les vacances – en famille ou avec ses amis?*)

- **range of sentence length/type and use of punctuation** (e.g. *Aller à la faculté après le lycée? Jamais!* or *Mes parents sont trop protecteurs, surtout mon père: 'ne sors pas toute seule en ville – c'est dangereux la nuit' dit-il!*)

- **structure/organisation** (introducing the general point before giving specific examples; paragraphs dealing with a specific side or aspect of the whole issue; conclusion to reflect on whole issue, etc.)

Student activity

Make a brief list of (three or four) possible presentation topics which you might consider for the Higher oral assessment. You will need to try to strike the right balance between being too general and too specific, in order to follow them up under the discussion part without resorting to repetition of ideas or content, while at the same time ensuring there is good quality language features in the presentation.

PART 3: EXEMPLARY MATERIALS

An example of a satisfactory oral assessment performance

Consider this example of an imaginary candidate's grade C performance in the oral assessment. Errors and clumsy expressions are underlined.

Go to the dedicated Higher French Grade Booster page on the Leckie and Leckie website to listen to the following presentation and discussion.

Presentation

Je vais vous parler de mes rapports domestiques chez moi. Tout d'abord, mes parents...

Généralement, je m'entends assez bien avec ma mère. Ma mère est institutrice dans une école primaire. Elle est très intelligente et bavarde. Ma mère est très sympa et je peux discuter avec ma mère quand j'ai un problème.

Mon père...Je ne m'entends pas bien avec mon père. Il s'appelle David et il a cinquante ans. Il est homme d'affaires, il travaille dans un bureau à Edimbourg. Mon père est très sévère. Il est pénible! Je ne peux pas sortir avec mes amis la semaine et je ne peux pas aller en vacances avec mes amies. Aussi, il est ennuyeux. Il regarde toujours les <u>actualities</u> à la télé.

J'ai un petit frère, John, il a douze ans. Je ne m'entends pas avec mon frère, parce qu'il prend toujours mes CDs. Mes parents préfèrent mon petit frère, il reçoit le même argent de poche que moi, <u>c'est ne</u> pas juste. Aussi, il est très paresseux. Je dois aider avec le ménage, mais John ne fait rien. Je range mes affaires, je sors la poubelle. Aussi, mon frère est très énervant, parce qu'il joue au foot tous les jours et il ne travaille pas.

En général, je m'entends assez bien avec ma mère mais pas bien avec mon père et mon frère. J'ai un petit ami et j'adore ça mais ma famille est difficile. C'est la vie!

Analysis

This is an accurate but limited presentation. On the one hand, the task is completed well enough – we understand everything that is communicated about the candidate's relationships with her family and, although she does not provide much at all in the way of explanation or reasoning, the meaning is generally conveyed clearly. The structure of the piece, which divides into separate paragraphs on her mother, father and younger brother, is successful and comprehensible, and there is even a recognisable introduction and conclusion. The candidate's command of the present tense is sound and convincing, and the use of modals (*je ne peux pas aller...; je dois aider...*) is competent. Opinions and reasons, however simple, are readily understood.

On the other hand, the range of both vocabulary and grammar is limited. The adjectives used to describe her family – *intelligent, bavard, sympa, pénible, ennuyeux, énervant* – are basic to say the least. The repeated use of *aussi* implies a list of points the candidate wishes to make about her family without the ability to express these in a rich and varied way. However, probably the most obvious sign of the limited nature of the French is the inability to link ideas within the same sentence: the two examples of *parce que...* are the sole attempts to provide coherence through conjunctions, and the norm is for short simple sentences (such as *Aussi il est ennuyeux. Il regarde toujours les actualités...*) rather than complex ones. Finally, although the task is satisfactorily completed, there are a few arguably irrelevant points – the contribution of the parents' jobs is a prime example – as though the candidate is scraping around for safe, over-rehearsed language.

6/10

Discussion

 Teacher: Eh bien, merci beaucoup, Laura. Parlons un peu plus de tes rapports avec tes parents. Ils ne veulent pas que tu partes en vacances avec tes amies, alors. Pourquoi?

Candidate: Oui...mon père est très stricte. Je ne peux pas aller en vacances avec mes amies en Espagne après mes examens.

Teacher: Pour quelles raisons exactement?

Candidate: Il pense (...) je suis trop jeune.

Teacher: Est-ce qu'il pense que c'est dangereux?

Candidate: Oui, c'est dangereux...mon père n'est pas content...il préfère les vacances en famille, mais selon moi, les vacances en famille, c'est ennuyeux.

Teacher: Et quand vous partez en vacances, en famille, comment c'est? L'année dernière, par exemple, qu'est-ce vous avez fait, toi et tes parents?

Candidate: *L'année dernière...?*

Teacher: *Oui, c'est ça. Parle-moi de tes vacances l'année dernière.*

Candidate: *L'année dernière, je suis allée en Italie avec ma famille. C'était très ennuyeux. J'ai détesté...*

Teacher: *Et qu'est-ce que vous avez fait en Italie?*

Candidate: *On a nagé dans la piscine, on a joué au tennis,...euh...j'ai acheté des souvenirs, j'ai allée dans un centre commercial...*

Teacher: *Oui...*

Candidate: *Euh...j'ai acheté des souvenirs pour mes amies en Ecosse, j'ai achéte un T-shirt, des cartes postales, j'ai mangé dans un restaurant, je n'aime pas, c'était affreux!*

Teacher: *Et le soir, alors, qu'est-ce qu'il y avait à faire?*

Candidate: *Le soir, oui, j'ai allée...je suis allée à la disco et j'ai écouté la musique pop. C'était super. Mais mon père resté dans le hôtel avec mon frère et ma mère. Mon père est très ennuyeux. C'est impossible.*

Teacher: *Mmmm...d'accord. Bon, tu as mentionné ton petit ami tout à l'heure. Il est comment? Quelles sont ses bonnes qualités, à ton avis?*

Candidate: *Ah oui, mon petit ami, il est génial. Il s'appelle John et il a vingt ans. Il est très grand et sportif. Il est les cheveux blonds. Il est sympa et intelligent. Il va à la université en Glasgow, à Glasgow.*

Teacher: *Et ton père s'entend bien avec ton petit ami?*

Candidate: *Euh...non, mon père déteste lui.*

Teacher: *Ton père ne s'entend pas bien avec John...peux-tu me dire pourquoi?*

Candidate: *Il pense (...) je suis trop jeune pour lui. Mon père est furieux quand je sorte en ville avec mon petit ami. Aussi, mon père déteste aller au pub et John adore ça. Il a une voiture et il sait faire. Il est travaille...non...il travaille dans un supermarché.*

Teacher: *Je comprends. Et en général, Laura, penses-tu que tu as assez de liberté à la maison?*

Candidate: *J'aime beaucoup mes parents mais je voudrais plus de liberté.*

Teacher: *Par exemple?*

Candidate: *Je voudrais sortir quand je veux, je voudrais aller à la disco, à la boum. J'ai voudrais rester avec mes amis, je voudrais...euh...*

Teacher: *Tu as quand même le droit de faire ce que tu veux de temps en temps?*

Candidate: *Je ne comprends pas. Répétez, s'il vous plaît?*

Teacher: *Tu as quand même le droit de sortir le week-end, par exemple?*

Candidate: Oui, mais je dois être à la maison à onze heures et demie et <u>c'est ne pas</u> juste.

Teacher: Bon, passons à autre chose…Discutons tes projets d'avenir après l'école. As-tu l'intention d'aller à la faculté?

Candidate: Oui, je voudrais aller à <u>la</u> université et étudier l'informatique. <u>C'est ça?</u>

Teacher: Pourquoi as-tu choisi de continuer avec l'informatique?

Candidate: Parce que j'adore ça. Et je suis forte en informatique. C'est ma matière préférée à l'école et ma prof est génial. Aussi, j'adore <u>le</u> ordinateurs, <u>c'est super.</u>

Teacher: Est-ce que tu as choisi l'université?

Candidate: Oui, Dundee est très bien. C'est une grande ville, il y a beaucoup de magasins et j'adore aller au cinéma tous les samedis. La grande ville, c'est plus intéressant.

Teacher: Et quel métier t'intéresse?

Candidate: J'aime…je voudrais travailler avec les ordinateurs. j'aimerais voyager en Afrique ou Amérique dans le futur.

Teacher: Qu'est-ce que tu aimerais faire en Amérique?

Candidate: New York est très, très bien. Et <u>Florida</u>, il fait chaud et je vais nager tous les jours à la plage. Et aussi, <u>les Américains, c'est sympa et beau</u>. C'est plus intéressant pour <u>jeunes personnes</u>.

Teacher: Et ton métier idéal, c'est quoi?

Candidate: Mon métier idéal…euh…c'est <u>(…)</u> actrice. Oui, je voudrais beaucoup d'argent et acheter une grande maison avec cinq chambres et une piscine. Et les films, c'est <u>très</u> super parce que c'est créatif et pas comme la vie <u>ennuyeux</u> de l'Ecosse.

Teacher: Bon, merci, Laura, je crois que nous avons terminé…

Analysis

This is a satisfactory performance, but no more. The task, which is basically to answer questions on topics related to the presentation subject of family relationships (in the lifestyles theme), and then to go on to answer questions which come from a second theme (in this case, holidays, from the wider world theme), has been coped with reasonably well. Firstly, the candidate is *'capable of coming to an understanding of all that is said'* (see the pegged marking criteria under the satisfactory section): for although she – we've called her Laura – occasionally doesn't grasp the meaning of what the teacher says, she manages to ask for it to be repeated until she has understood.

It is worth learning a couple of phrases which will allow the teacher to repeat or explain further, and avoid either embarrassing silences or a wrong answer! *Je ne comprends pas. Vous pouvez répétez, s'il vous plait?* works well when under duress!

Secondly, Laura is generally able to communicate, as her grasp of grammar is sufficient *'to convey meaning clearly'*, in spite of some errors. The grammar is certainly not fancy: the vast majority is in the present tense, while there is a small section in the past tense, where she talks of what she did on holiday last year (*j'ai acheté des souvenirs; j'ai mangé dans un restaurant; je suis allée à la disco*); the future is communicated by the repetitive but accurate use of *je voudrais* plus an infinitive, when discussing her plans for university and jobs/holidays.

Limited as all this is, it demonstrates *'sufficient accuracy'* through tense use. Other structures are also relevant to the satisfactory mark here: for instance, she can express opinion and provide reasons, such as when she complains that her father feels that she is *trop jeune* for holidays alone with her friends, or indeed to have a boyfriend. At times Laura's French is a little faulty (*c'est ne pas juste* is her opinion of having an 11.30 curfew) or simplistic (she wishes to take a degree in computing because IT is her *matière préférée*). But the main point is that we *understand* easily what she says. Even if her French is downright clumsy, as in her reason for wishing to be an actress when older, Laura manages to get across her feeling that it offers her a more creative outlet than her present dull existence in Scotland!

That said, there are weaknesses in the Discussion which restrict the mark to the satisfactory. Chief among these is the limited range of grammar and vocabulary. As in the presentation, there are times here when you wonder just how far she has progressed from Standard Grade or Intermediate 2. The description of the boyfriend is a good example: she gives simple information about him, using very basic language (*il est très grand et sportif; il s'appelle John et il a vingt ans*, etc.) which really doesn't develop into a mature or insightful response. This is clearly the level Laura feels most comfortable with, as we see repeated examples of this limited, quite mundane approach to discussion (as with her description of Dundee, what she would like to do in her free time, and so on). The repeated use of very basic vocabulary (*ennuyeux; sympa; grand; intelligent; super; génial*, etc.) means that this candidate could never be said to possess the *'wide range'* we read about in the good criteria.

And then there is the question of accuracy, which is generally sound but shows cracks on several occasions, such as the use of *penser* without *que*, the absence of the direct object as in *j'ai détesté* (and the botched attempt at *mon père déteste lui*), the confused word order with the negative (*ce n'est pas juste*), the forgotten liaison of *l'* before a vowel sound (*la université, le hôtel,* etc.), and so on. The effect of this is to undermine the reliability of the accuracy as a whole, and to suggest that Laura's grasp of the basics is fragile. It is certainly true to say that, if the ideas are as simple and as undeveloped as Laura's are here, then any significant mistakes are going to make it impossible to achieve a level beyond Satisfactory. The lack of depth and length of the discussion also might suggest limited ambition on the part of the candidate, and it is worth considering this if your intention is to reach beyond a grade C.

> No one mentions words like 'interesting' in the pegged marking criteria, but it is worth pointing out that 'interest value' does have some weight – it demonstrates the desire to go beyond the basics, and this in itself usually produces vocabulary and grammar of a higher level than a grade C.

Finally, we should take a look at Laura's *idiom* – just how French does her French sound? I am not talking of her accent or intonation or pronunciation, all of which, again, are *'sufficient to be understood by a sympathetic speaker'*, but rather of *the way she chooses to express herself.* She plans to continue her computing studies because *le ordinateurs, c'est super;* she adores Americans – presumably American men! – because *c'est sympa et beau.* This is French as it is never spoken, and is a perfect illustration of why you ought to be preparing thoroughly for your discussion by ensuring that your phrases and expressions are the kind uttered by an actual French person. Remember, you can check your phrases and expressions with your teacher or French Assistant at any time during the build-up to your oral assessment, so that what you come out with on the day sounds…well, *French!*

9/15

An example of a very good oral assessment performance

Go to the dedicated Higher French Grade Booster page to listen to the following presentation and discussion.

Presentation

Les images stéréotypées des habitudes culinaires et la question de la santé en Ecosse et en France, est le sujet de ma présentation…

On se plaint souvent dans les médias que nous, les Britanniques, et surtout les Ecossais, devrions faire plus d'effort en ce qui concerne la santé en général: c'est-à-dire qu'on devrait manger mieux, boire moins d'alcool, renoncer à fumer, participer à des activités sportives plus régulièrement. Mais qu'est-ce que cela voudrait dire, exactement, être en bonne santé?

Tout d'abord, examinons la question de la cuisine chez nous en Ecosse. Beaucoup d'Ecossais aiment manger le 'fish and chips', ou poisson-frites, avec de la sauce et du sel, emballé dans un journal. Moi, par exemple, je trouve sympa de manger ça en revenant d'un match de foot le samedi après-midi avec mes copains. Ce n'est pas cher et c'est rapide, et ça sent tellement bon, n'est-ce pas? Et nous avons l'habitude d'aller au snack ou au McDo pendant l'heure du déjeuner à midi, car il faut faire la queue à la cantine et attendre longtemps. En plus, la nourriture à l'école est vraiment affreuse. Puis c'est normal de bouffer une pizza devant la télé le soir, en buvant son coca ou – encore pire – une boite d'Irn Bru. C'est comme ça qu'on mange en Ecosse: tout est sucré, gras, malsain. Nous mangeons pour remplir un trou.

Au contraire, les Français, eux, mangent comme il faut, car ils prennent leur temps à manger au lieu de le faire le plus vite possible. En France, on mange tous ensemble en famille et la nourriture est bonne. Selon les images stéréotypées, les Français mangent des escargots et des cuisses de grenouille tous les jours, mais en réalité ils prennent beaucoup de fruits et de légumes et moins de produits sucrés ou de matières grasses. Au collège, c'est plus sain aussi: les crudités, par exemple, on ne les voit pas en Ecosse, mais en France les élèves les mangent volontiers et avec plaisir. Tandis que nous mangeons pour vivre, les Français, eux, vivent pour manger. Cela représente aussi un mode de vie tout à fait différent entre les deux pays.

Analysis

This is clearly a very good performance in the presentation section, and fulfils all of the requirements as set out in the pegged marking criteria. From the start, the candidate (Michael) displays a very confident handling of language through the advanced and complex title, promising to deal with the comparison of eating habits in France and Scotland, but also touching on the wider issues of health and lifestyle, too. This will cleverly allow for that wider Discussion topic to be developed later on in the oral assessment.

The main feature which impresses is the range of vocabulary and grammar, for although the actual points the candidate is making are not new – after all, he is talking about the *images stéréotypées* – they are presented with confidence and variety. For instance, we hear about the way the Scots generally are portrayed in the media, but also of the specific things Michael does in his own life that support such a view. Rather than allow for the presentation to degenerate into a kind of horrible history treatment of how unhealthy the Scots are by giving a long list of food and drink items responsible for our poor health, the candidate engages the listener on a more personal level by exposing his own routines of eating his fish and chips on the way home from football at the weekend. This shows how the topic has been considered, processed, personalised, and not just mindlessly mugged up from a textbook. Yet the topic does not stay within the comfort zone of Michael's own eating habits, for we are then drawn back to a more general picture of Scots pupils' trips to fast food joints and from there to the nation's dependence as a whole on the unhealthiest diet imaginable.

This shifting from the wider argument to the specific is also a feature of the treatment of how the French eat, and forces Michael to demonstrate his ability to use (simple) verbs in the third person plural (*les Français mangent/prennent*), the use of *on* as a general pronoun (*on mange tous ensemble*), before going on to focus on the actual food eaten by pupils at a French school. It also involves the language of comparison (*au contraire, les Français, eux,*) before contrasting the two nationalities' attitudes to food and life in the final sentences.

If you look closely at the actual vocabulary, much of it is remarkably straightforward, especially when discussing what people actually eat and drink. But the real achievement is how effortlessly the candidate moves from one level of the topic to another and in doing so never has to repeat himself. The style of language varies with the different perspectives taken, from general to personal, formal to informal, from statement to question, factual to opinion-based. This is evidence of excellent control and manipulation of language.

10/10

Discussion

 Teacher: Dis-moi, Michael, qu'est-ce que tu fais pour rester en bonne santé?

Candidate: Eh bien, moi, j'essaie de manger relativement bien, par exemple pendant la semaine je préfère apporter des sandwichs au lieu de manger à la cantine, parce que ça me permet de sélectionner moi-même ce que je mange. Et à la maison je prépare de temps en temps le repas du soir – du poulet ou du poisson avec du riz ou des pates, toujours avec des légumes frais – et je prends régulièrement un fruit. Comme ça, il y a toujours la source de protéines, de vitamines qu'il faut.

Teacher: Et tu pratiques du sport aussi?

Candidate: Oui, assez souvent. Je fais partie de l'équipe de foot au lycée. Je m'entraine <u>tous</u> les mercredis et il y a un match presque <u>tous</u> les semaines le samedi après-midi. C'est bien pour se maintenir en forme. Mais ma passion, c'est le cyclisme et je fais du vélo avec mon père pratiquement tous les soirs...

Teacher: Tu participes aux concours?

Candidate: Cette année, non, car j'ai trop de devoirs. Je vais passer mes examens au mois de juin et il faut que je travaille beaucoup. Mais l'année dernière, je faisais des courses cyclistes deux ou trois fois par mois. J'ai gagné une médaille d'or. Le sport, à mon avis, c'est un bon moyen de rester en pleine forme.

Teacher: Penses-tu qu'il y a un problème de la consommation d'alcool dans ta ville?

Candidate: Ah oui, absolument. Tous mes amis boivent le week-end, car il n'y a pas grand-chose à faire là ou j'habite. Nous n'avons pas de cinéma, pas de disco, pas de centre de loisirs chez nous. Alors on boit. C'est triste. Il y a aussi la question de la drogue, mais je ne comprends pas pourquoi on se drogue. C'est stupide et c'est dangereux.

Teacher: Quelle est la solution, à ton avis?

Candidate: Je ne sais pas. C'est une question difficile. Je n'ai pas <u>une</u> solution.

Teacher: Est-ce que tu fumes, Michael?

Candidate: Non, je ne fume pas parce que c'est très mauvais pour la santé. Le tabac est mauvais et on risque le cancer. En plus, c'est cher et je n'ai pas beaucoup d'argent.

Teacher: Et alors pourquoi les jeunes commencent-ils à fumer?

Candidate: Pourquoi? Parce que c'est adulte de fumer et leurs amis fument. Mon père fumait quand il était plus jeune. Mais maintenant il ne fume pas, il fait du vélo avec moi. Il a acheté un <u>nouvel</u> vélo avec l'argent et ma mère est très contente.

Teacher: Tu disais tout à l'heure qu'il n'y avait pas beaucoup de divertissements là ou tu habitais, mais tu habites à la campagne, n'est-ce pas, Michael? Trouves-tu qu'il y a des avantages d'habiter à la campagne?

Candidate: Ah oui, absolument. Il y a beaucoup d'avantages de la vie campagnarde. Tout d'abord, on n'a pas les inconvénients da la vie urbaine, car en ville c'est trop bruyant, il y plus de voitures, il y a trop de gens, et c'est très pollué…

Teacher: Mais tu préfères la vie de la campagne…?

Candidate: Oui, effectivement. Premièrement, c'est calme et c'est propre. Et puis on peut sortir en sécurité, même la nuit. D'<u>une</u> côté, on dit qu'il n'y a rien à faire, mais on est plus près de la nature et on peut se détendre plus facilement. Moi, je suis pour la vie campagnarde parce que la qualité de vie est supérieure.

Teacher: Mais que fais-tu pendant ton temps libre?

Candidate: Je me promène avec mon chien tous les jours, je monte à cheval assez souvent.

Teacher: Mais on n'a pas tout ce qu'il faut pour s'amuser: aucune boite, aucun cinéma…

Candidate: Oui, c'est vrai. Et les transports en commun ne sont pas bons. Et mes amis habitent au centre-ville, donc c'est inconvénient de temps en temps. Mais en général, je pense que la vie ici est plus agréable et moins sale. Ma soeur ainée habite à Londres parce qu'elle travaille pour une agence commerciale et je trouve que c'est vraiment stressant là-bas. Lorsque j'ai visité ma soeur en été j'ai trouvé que tout le monde était pressé et agressif.

Teacher: Elle fait quoi comme métier, ta soeur?

Candidate: Elle travaille pour une agence de publicité depuis cinq ou six ans maintenant. Elle travaille à Londres, mais elle voyage beaucoup aussi – l'année dernière au mois de décembre elle est allée à New York avec ses collègues et au mois d'avril elle a passé quelques jours en Italie. Elle adore son travail, parce qu'elle est créative et aime le contact avec les gens.

Teacher: Et cela te dirait, ce genre de travail?

Candidate: Je ne sais pas. Je ne voudrais pas habiter dans une grande ville polluée et bruyante; je préférerais vivre à la campagne comme vétérinaire, par exemple, et travailler en plein air. En plus, j'adore les animaux, donc ce serait un bon métier pour moi.

Teacher: Tes parents travaillent tous les deux?

Candidate: Oui, mon père est médecin à l'hôpital et ma mère est infirmière en ville.

Teacher: Et avant de trouver un emploi plus permanent, tu as l'intention de voyager, de voir le monde?

Candidate: Oui, j'aimerais passer une année sabbatique en Afrique à faire du travail bénévole, peut-être dans une école primaire. Je voudrais travailler avec les enfants. J'ai toujours eu l'intention de visiter l'Afrique et je crois que ce serait une expérience incroyable.

Teacher: Une dernière question, Michael: y a-t-il un métier que tu ne pourrais jamais faire, un emploi que tu ne supporterais pas?

Candidate: Ah oui, bien sur! Il y en a beaucoup! Je ne pourrais jamais être politicien, car je trouve l'idée de la vie politique insupportable. Et je déteste les médias, alors pour moi cela serait <u>une</u> désastre. Et je n'aimerais pas devenir employé d'une banque puisque je m'ennuie très vite et je suis nul en mathématiques. Mais le pire pour moi serait de travailler sans cesse avec les ordinateurs. J'ai horreur de ça!

Teacher: Bon, merci.

Analysis

This is without question a very good performance. The most striking feature is the candidate's willingness and ability to give extended answers and *'readily go beyond minimal responses'*. From the very start, when asked how he made sure of leading a healthy lifestyle, Michael provides a detailed reply, with specific examples of the sandwiches he makes and why, and goes on, *unprompted,* to explain that he cooks occasionally at home, backing up his meals with scientific evidence! This is just one example of many such instances of the candidate's initiative and enterprising approach to the task, and accounts for the hugely varied subject matter he covers – from eating habits, sport and drink problems in today's youth to a lively debate between life in town versus life in the country, the various types of employment in his family, his own future intentions and finally an explanation of three jobs he would hate and why.

It is easy to overlook the fact that it is the candidate's good French, as well as his attitude, that earns him the marks. It is the way he is able to move across the tenses that secures the feeling in the examiner that he is highly competent – and confident, obviously – in his present, past and future tense work. Take the example of his reply to the question about competitive cycling, where he explains that he has too much on this year (*j'ai trop de devoirs*; and the subjunctive *il faut que je travaille*), followed by his reasoning of future exams (*je vais passer mes examens…*), before contrasting this with life last year, where he repeatedly entered competitions (hence the imperfect in *je faisais des courses cyclistes*), finally ending with his one-off cycling success in the perfect tense (*j'ai gagné une médaille d'or*) – he even manages to return to the present tense at the end of this response in order to share with us his general view of sport's contribution to good health (*le sport… c'est un bon moyen de rester en pleine forme*).

The switching of tenses is accompanied by regular but varied use of time phrases (*cette année, cet été, l'année dernière,* etc.) as well as comfortable turns of phrase and sentences of different types and length. The candidate's ability to express himself *comfortably* and *confidently* is also found in the small but repeated additional details he fits in to his replies: words like *relativement, régulièrement, absolument, effectivement* are sprinkled very naturally on top of his answers. Even when uncertain of a solution to the drugs problem, the candidate has the wit and grasp of French to sound authoritative. (*Je ne sais pas. C'est une question difficile.*) But the number of errors is also significantly small (see underlinings), and there is nothing more important in working towards a grade A mark than sustained accuracy.

15/15

Student activity

Go back to the quality language checklist, and draft out a mini paragraph containing four to five of the features. This will concentrate your thoughts on writing at Higher level rather than reproducing Credit/Intermediate 2 level of language. The basic underlying principle must be to create positive impact with the level and richness of your written and spoken French at each opportunity.

2 Reading Comprehension and Translation

Part 1: General

Part 2: Reading comprehension

Part 3: Translation

PART 1: GENERAL

Paper I is actually called Reading and Directed Writing. It lasts 1 hour 40 minutes, and is worth a total of 45 marks. As we are told in the Arrangement Documents, this is sub divided into:

Part A – Reading (55 minutes, 30 marks)

- *Reading comprehension, involving written answers to questions in English (20 marks), followed by a translation into English (10 marks). One passage of approximately 550–650 words will be set, related to the prescribed themes. A glossary will be provided and use of a dictionary is permitted.*

Part B – Directed Writing (45 minutes, 15 marks)

- *Directed writing task, based on a scenario given in English. Candidates will be required to provide specific information in a piece of writing of 150–180 words. Use of a dictionary is permitted.*

Firstly, it is important to point out that parts A and B have nothing in common, other than that they are both parts of the Higher French examination – they are bundled together to make up Paper I for convenience. We will keep them separate in this book because it makes more sense to show you what skills and knowledge are required for the reading part first.

Secondly, you need to be aware that, although it might seem almost an afterthought, the translation piece is worth 10/30 marks of part A. This may strike you as a little disproportionate, since the bulk of your time and efforts appear to be required to answer the comprehension questions (20/30), but an awareness of the marks allocation is an essential feature of being well prepared.

Let us look at the reading comprehension and translation parts in that order.

PART 2: READING COMPREHENSION

The most obvious thing about the actual passage – and there is only a *single* passage – is its length and therefore its depth of detail. If you have worked your way through Credit reading at Standard Grade, then you will be used to four or five reading passages, covering a variety of topics, of approximately 80–200 words each. If you have sat your Intermediate 2 exam, then you will have tackled a reading paper of four to five texts, ranging from 50–300 words in length. But at Higher level, the SQA are clear about their intentions to 'extend' the candidate's ability to read and to get to grips properly with an in-depth article. As we are told in the National Course Specification details, this means:

'With the help of a dictionary, obtain factual information, ideas and opinions, with (…) detail and accuracy, from text of some complexity likely to be encountered in personal, social or vocational life, relating to the prescribed themes and topic areas.'

The reading passage at Higher is the type you would expect to find in a magazine or newspaper article that tackles a topical issue in a fairly serious way, in as much as it is an in-depth text, formally written, which can cover both general and personal perspectives.

In this respect, revising for the reading comprehension in your Higher English by ensuring you read at least one major article from a serious newspaper or other publication once a week is good practice as it covers similar ground and involves many of the same skills as are required for the reading comprehension in Higher French.

It would be wrong, however, to expect a nice, clear-cut, all-about-one-topic article to appear in your Higher French reading paper. The SQA are determined to use passages that cut across the prescribed themes and topics, demanding a level of maturity beyond that required in reading a passage with narrow focus. So what we are faced with is a combination of depth and breadth, more exacting than you experience in the reading NAB, and which will necessitate a considerable amount of extended reading during the Higher course. (We will return later to some useful sources for reading practice.) A look at the so-called topic areas of the reading passages in the Higher French examination over the last few years will prove this point.

2001

Rien à foot, tes études d'abord! This magazine article is about Mélanie Charpentier, a mother who is worried about the future career of Cédric, her gifted son.

In fact this article covers family relationships, the world of work, daily routine, as well as the boy's obsession with the beautiful game!

2002

Avec la course à pied, il sauve des vies humaines! This magazine article is about Alain Gestin, who devotes his life to raising money for charity.

This covers such diverse issues as past jobs, personal accident, orphans in Senegal, in addition to charity work.

2003

'The Gap Year' This magazine article is about the 'gap year' which many French students like to spend in Britain.

The article touches on student life and life in London, but in fact spends more time describing how the organisation that arranges gap years actually works, before going on to discuss the pros and cons of the gap year itself.

2004

Un Trekking au Népal: Le voyage d'une Vie A French travel writer tells us how to make the most of a once-in-a lifetime holiday, hiking in the Himalayan mountain range in remote Nepal.

This article is a highly descriptive account of life in a very different part of the world, with emphasis on the physical environment and the experiences of adventure tourism in an extraordinary setting. This is the most narrowly focused reading passage in Higher French to date.

2005

Mendiants d'Internet This article tells us how the Internet can be used for begging, as well as for job-hunting.

Among the topics covered here are: job-hunting; how to get money for nothing; describing young people; earning money; information technology.

2006

Une nouvelle vie en France This article discusses the reasons why people from Britain are moving to France.

Also covered are cultural comparisons, lifestyle descriptions, the role of television programmes in this trend and perspectives of life in the Languedoc region.

2007

Dialoguer en famille... Quelle corvée! This passage states that families talk less to one another nowadays, and examines the reasons why.

Within this article we cover areas such as family relationships, the mindset of adolescents, the role of television, the interfering nature of mobile phones, rules and regulations in the home, and a proposal to establish a domestic contract in the search for peace in the home.

2008

Comment mon blog a changé ma vie. In this passage, Camille describes how her blog (her online diary) changed her life.

This article covers areas such as information technology, celebrity status, diary writing and journalism.

The major themes and topics are, therefore:

- the world of work
- holidays

with a particular focus on student life.

Clearly, these passages require a sound working knowledge of the key topic vocabulary and an awareness of the register and tone of the language, moving from informal and conversational to factual and highly formal. So, while the dictionary can help us with a basic vocabulary translation, we still need to concentrate hard to follow the narrative point of view.

However, it is easy to overlook the important fact that these articles require an ability to understand the most challenging aspect of Higher French grammar: tenses. It is *the way these passages switch from one tense to another* that creates the greatest challenge for the reader, and they do so very often *without the signposting of helpful time phrases.*

Year	Grammar
2001	Present, perfect, imperfect, future, conditional tenses.
2002	Present, perfect, imperfect tenses.
2003	Present, imperfect, future tenses.
2004	Present, perfect, imperfect, future tenses.
2005	Present, perfect, imperfect, future, conditional tenses.
2006	Present, perfect, imperfect, future tenses.
2007	Present, perfect and imperfect tenses; commands.
2008	Present, perfect, imperfect, future tenses.

In addition to the variety of tenses, there is constant use of modal verbs (*on peut voyager…; si vous voulez passer…; vous devez absolument embaucher…*, etc.), two verbs together (*j'ai appris à piloter…; je n'allais pas tenter…*), difficult verbs like *falloir,* often with a negative (*il ne faudrait pas croire cependant…*) or not (*il faut être alerte tout le temps*), and so on.

In short, you are being tested on how much French grammar, as well as vocabulary and phraseology, you have learned, as there is no way you could possibly look up more than the 10–20 key words of the text in the dictionary. Although you are not given advance warning of the actual topics that will come up in the reading comprehension, the passage tests your knowledge of individual words and how meanings are created by a collection of these words. Increasing the words and phrases you are familiar with the first step towards improving your reading skills. This should be warning enough to commit a serious amount of time at home, from the summer holidays onwards, learning these.

Leckie and Leckie's own *Higher French Course Notes* is the best summary of topic and theme vocabulary, phrases and grammar-through-sentences that I have come across. It is particularly valuable because you can use it on your own – it is superbly set out for private study – and come away having learned a great deal. It is no surprise that one of the authors is the Principal Assessor of Higher French examinations!

Student activity

It is a priority to be able to recognise the different tenses of verbs. The most helpful approach to this is to draw up a hit list of the top 30–40 verbs in French, across the main tenses (imperfect/perfect/present/future/conditional), using the third person singular. You could expand this table, for instance, adopting an alphabetical system.

Infinitive	Imperfect	Perfect	Present	Future	Conditional
aller	allait	est allé(e)	va	ira	irait
arriver	arrivait	est arrivé(e)	arrive	arrivera	arriverait
avoir	avait	a eu	a	aura	aurait
boire	buvait	a bu	boit	boira	boirait

The next thing to look at is how the SQA use this paper to assess your reading skills – in other words, how they test your ability to put your knowledge of grammar, vocabulary and phrases into action in tackling a task. There are some general points to make about the comprehension questions, and these are true for all papers to date.

- The *number of marks* available for each question is given in brackets; this strongly suggests how many specific points you have to make to gain full marks per question.

- The questions are in *chronological order* of the passage itself.

- There are some questions which test your understanding in a simple, vocabulary-based way (often beginning with *what…?*).

- There are other questions demanding that you show an understanding of *how* and *why* something has happened.

- Some questions explicitly ask you to *explain* how a certain situation has developed.

Looking at the above, it should be clear that the way you express yourself is key, as you are being asked to demonstrate comprehension and explain how meaning is created in the text. While there is no need to write in full sentences all the time, you must demonstrate a complete understanding which requires no work or sympathy from the marker. After all, you are not under the same kind of time pressure here as you will be later on in the listening comprehension, so a completely intelligible answer is always necessary.

A quick look at the answers to the reading comprehension questions at the back of the Leckie and Leckie *Past Papers* booklet gives an immediate insight into the SQA demands in this respect – these are, after all, the official SQA answers!

Time and time again, the Higher French examination report complains that poor expression in English, inadequate detail and answers only implying rather explicitly stating what is required are major reasons for candidates' under-performance in this paper.

Carrying on with the theme of reading comprehension skills, it is a good time to round up the essential dos and don'ts in this part of paper I:

Dos

✔ *Read through the English preamble and questions first, as these form a sort of summary of the whole text.*

✔ *Examine the general passage title and the paragraph titles.*

✔ *Spend adequate time ensuring you have a general understanding of the passage as a whole before worrying about specifics – remember, the gist of the text's meaning is a prerequisite to detailed comprehension.*

✔ *Always attempt to answer all the questions in turn.*

✔ *Check over the number of different points you make in each answer and ensure nothing relevant to the answer is left out. (You will only be penalised for extra information if it casts serious doubt on whether you have really understood.)*

✔ *Show understanding by explaining yourself with reference to the text – persuade, convince and give proof in this way.*

Don'ts

✗ *Give vague answers or limit your answers to the minimum – you are not awarded marks for speaking the truth, but for demonstrating understanding through specific detail.*

✗ *Become over-reliant on the dictionary, especially as there will be words in the text which may not be relevant to any of the questions.*

✗ *Ever just translate.*

✗ *Hedge your bets by giving an either/or answer.*

✗ *Expect marks to be given for correct information in the wrong place or under the wrong answer. (Markers are under strict instruction not to accept this.)*

Interestingly, the instructions given to markers of this paper often repeat many of the above points. For instance, markers are told that *'no points can be awarded in a sentence whose meaning is unclear'* and *'the inclusion of irrelevant information in an answer should not be penalised unless it contradicts the text'*, so there is plenty of evidence to support the tips given above. It should be clear from all this that the reading comprehension is really testing your ability to answer questions properly and demonstrate your understanding of the passage.

The **2008 reading comprehension** illustrates the points made here (This paper is not included in this book, so you would do well to find a copy). It concerns Camille's experience of writing her blog, but is more concerned with the writing process, her experience of online 'fame' and her emotions and aspirations than the world of information technology.

The opening paragraph lays down the challenge of the piece right away by using imperfect, future, perfect and present tenses, all in the space of seven lines. The passage as a whole is demanding because of the way it jumps about from one aspect of her blogging to another, and the reader has to try hard to follow the thread as it weaves from place to place (New York to Paris), from person to person (Andy Warhol to her friend, Anuja, to Bruno, Elodie and Honorée who have responded to Camille's daily diary) and from one publication to another (*La Gazette new-yorkaise* to the *Daily Telegraph* to the *Gazette parisienne*). Even the writing process covers the diversity of the narrator's own work, referring us to her articles on the van Gogh exposition at the Metropolitan, the pros and cons of New York as the host city for the 2012 Olympics and the policing of the streets of Harlem.

In addition, the perspective is constantly shifting from the personal and private (as in Camille's own feelings of doubt, joy and achievement) to the impersonal and public (*les statistiques de visiteurs à mon blog*). In short, it is difficult to keep track of where this article is taking us!

It is all the more important, therefore, to use whatever guides to the text there are. Clearly the subtitles of **Me and the City** and **Attention au blog!** give us vague indications that the text in these sections will cover life in New York and the highs and lows of blogging respectively; the final subtitle **Je suis devenue blog-addict!** reflects the intensity of Camille's blog experiences. More of a guide, however, are the comprehension questions – as already mentioned, these follow the order of the passage strictly, and can form a useful summary of the text in English. These should be read even before you skim over the article for the first time.

Fortunately, each question begins with a general statement, before asking you specific questions, and in so doing gives you the lines to concentrate on when answering. Finally, the number of marks available are to be found opposite each individual question. Remember that these marks suggest the number of pieces of information you are expected to provide in your answer.

Now let us look at the actual questions, and consider what the best answers would be.

NOTE: under the acceptable answers, underlinings denote essential features.

1. A large number of blogs (...) have sprung up since 1999.   (lines 1–17)

   (a) What prompted Camille to start her blog?   **1 point**

   Acceptable answers
   – *(pure) jealousy*
   OR
   – *she saw her friend's blog/her friend had started one*

   Unacceptable answers
   – *to become famous*
   OR
   – *she was jealous of other people's blogs*

   (b) How had Anuja tried to make her blog immediately attractive?   **2 points**

   Acceptable answers
   – *by creating an elegant home-page (or equivalent)*
   – *(in the photo) she appears well made-up <u>and</u> with a broad smile (both details)*

   Unacceptable answers
   – *by showing a photo of the beach (misreading of page as plage)*
   – *by showing a photo on her blog*
   – *she had too much make-up (missing the point that the make-up was attractive)*
   – *she had a fake smile (whereas in fact her smile was viewed as an advantage)*

2. On her blog, Camille writes about her life in New York.   (lines 18–48)

   (a) Give details of the kinds of thing that Camille puts on her blog.   **3 points**

   Acceptable answers (any 3 from 5)
   – *life as a <u>university student</u> of <u>journalism</u>*
   – *a review of a van Gogh <u>exhibition/exposition</u>*
   – *questioning New York's bid to host the 2012 Olympics*
   – *meeting the police patrol on the streets of Harlem (must get both meeting police and where)*
   – *photos illustrating each article*

Unacceptable answers
- *writes about art exhibitions/van Gogh (without any explanation)*
- *Youth Games (misreading of jeux as jeunes)*
- *her collision with a police patrol (without mention of her meeting or where)*
- *photos or illustrations (without explaining that they are for each article)*

(b) Why, in her opinion, do her readers find her site interesting?   **1 point**

Acceptable answers (any one from...)
- <u>the French</u> love New York
OR
- <u>the French</u> like/are interested in <u>everything to do with</u> New York
OR
- she gives/brings them some of the New York atmosphere/ambiance

Unacceptable answers
- *the French like to know about/be in touch with/stay in contact with New York*
- *they love it because it has a touch/feeling of New York*
- *... a taste of New York life (without mention of the fact that the French love the city)*

(c) Why did Bruno think her site was great?   **1 point**

Acceptable answers
- her descriptions of her <u>nights out/parties/evenings</u> give people a slice/glimpse of/an insight into New York life

Unacceptable answers
- *outings (with no reference to an insight into life in New York)*
- *things that happen at night*

(d) How does Camille react to comments such as this?   **1 point**

Acceptable answers (one answer from...)
- she is flattered/her ego is flattered/it boosts her ego
- she thought/thinks herself a superstar of the Internet

Unacceptable answers
- *she wants to be an Internet superstar*

3. There are also dangers in having your own blog.   (lines 49–67)

(a) What did Camille realise is a dangerous thing to do?   **1 point**

Acceptable answers
– *give personal/private details/details of her private life to strangers/to whoever (can read them)/to anyone you don't know/for the public to see on the Internet (the key idea here is giving **private details** to a **stranger**)*

Unacceptable answers
– *give details of private life on blog (without reference to strangers)*

(b) What happened after Camille gave Elodie the information that she asked for? **3 points**

Acceptable answers (any 3 from…)
– *that wasn't enough (for Elodie)/Elodie wanted more details*
OR
– *Elodie sent numerous/five emails to Camille/Elodie constantly sent emails to Camille*
– *Camille broke off contact/stopped replying*
– *Elodie's tone became less friendly/warm/hearty/cordial*
OR
– *she subjected Camille to a flood/torrent/wave/amount of abuse/insults/ threats*

Unacceptable answers
– *she sent five people emails*
– *she asked her to stop/she deleted her contact/she blocked her emails*
– *she became less polite (no mention of who was the culprit or victim)*
– *she (Camille) still suffers*
– *hate mail/she was nasty to her/she insulted her (again, no mention of who)*

4. Camille's blog has had a major impact upon her life.   (lines 68–94)

(a) Why did a journalist from the Daily Telegraph contact her? **2 points**

Acceptable answers
– *he read her/a review/report of /blog/comment(s)/remarks/commentary on a film/Les Choristes*
– *he had/wanted to interview the star and wanted to talk to her (both details needed)*

Unacceptable answers
– *to comment on her blog*
– *to propose a film*
– *he had interviewed the star (i.e. candidate thinks it has happened)*
– *he wanted her to interview the star (confusion of roles)*

– the star of the film wanted to talk to her
–... and he wanted her to speak/translate

(b) What eventual benefit did this bring to Camille?   **1 point**

Acceptable answers
  – she received a job <u>offer/offer</u> of employment/a (steady) job/work
  – the journalist/he <u>offered</u> her a job

Unacceptable answers
  – job offers (with no mention of Camille)
  – frequent work

(c) What shows how far Camille has become addicted to her blog?   **3 points**

Acceptable answers (any 3 from 4)
  – she checks the visitor/viewer statistics/statistics of visits to her blog/
   how many people have been on/visited/viewed the blog compulsively
   checks her blog as soon as she wakes up/first thing/gets up
  – she hates days when no one leaves/makes a comment/people don't
   comment/when she doesn't get comments/remarks
  – she is delighted when a new reader appears/come forward/joins her
   blog/is evident/arises/shows themselves/turns up/leaves a comment
  – she continually improves/doesn't stop/never stops improving her blog

Unacceptable answers
  – her blog statistics (without mention of her checking)
  – people don't do commentaries/people who don't leave comments (this
   implies a personal hatred)
  – a new lecture/lecturer (misunderstanding of word 'lecteur')

(d) Why does she describe herself as arrogant?   **1 point**

Acceptable answers
  – she thinks that <u>her readers</u> will be inconsolable/devastated/distraught
   if/when/that she stops/she goes back to France/she is leaving/her blog
   ends/without her blog

Unacceptable answers
 – readers are inconsolable (without saying why)
 – readers find <u>her</u> inconsolable (confusion about who is inconsolable)

Students should appreciate the importance of regularly practising reading at
this level, where the reader is exposed to a serious treatment of topical issues

and where the link to the Higher French syllabus might only be implicit rather than specifically related to one of the three themes. Below is a short – and by no means complete – list of useful reading resources which are intended specifically to support French Higher candidates develop the necessary reading skills.

- Higher Still Development Unit Reading comprehension articles, which your teacher will almost certainly be using in class or for homework, and which contain very useful language exercises.

- The more advanced versions of these, where a glossary is given to offer you extra support. (Particularly aimed at A/B candidates, and good for revision towards the end of the course or theme.)

- Past papers (Leckie and Leckie *Past Papers* give comprehensive marking schemes as issued by the SQA).

- Leckie and Leckie's *Higher French Course Notes* concentrate on essential phrases and vocabulary rather than actual full reading passages, but this is a reminder that longer articles are made up of a collection of expressions you will be expected to cover during the course.

- *How to Pass Higher French* (Hodder Gibson) gives some useful examples of both the NAB and external exam level of reading passages, and looks at candidate answers of varying degrees of ability.

- Both the Intermediate 1/Intermediate 2 and the Advanced Higher French reading programmes, written by the National Qualifications Curriculum Support team and published by Learning and Teaching Scotland, are excellent private study booklets because of the variety of length and difficulty of the texts they include and because of the very helpful information in the answer booklets regarding marking schemes.

In addition to these specifically French Higher targeted resources, I have found the following commercial publications useful in helping my own students over the years:

- *Au Point* (Nelson Thornes)
- *Vécu* (Hodder and Stoughton)
- *Arc-en-ciel 3 & 4* (Mary Glasgow Publications)
- *Points de Vue* (Mary Glasgow Publications)
- Mary Glasgow Publications magazines, particularly *Jeunes*
- *Métro pour l'Ecosse* (rouge) (Heinemann)
- *Authentik*
- Internet news in brief (Actualités)

It is important to remember that you are not just concerned with reading *practice*, but with improving and building on your vocabulary and grammar, and therefore every session you dedicate to extra reading should to produce *a list of 10–20 new words and 5–6 points of grammar or examples of tense work* that will take your general comprehension on a stage further. Otherwise you might feel that you have nothing to show for the additional work you've put in!

PART 3: TRANSLATION

It is tempting to think of the translation part as less important, especially since so much time and effort are spent on the reading comprehension, but try to remember that the translation, even if it is only a few lines in length, is still worth 10/30 points in this paper, and 10% of the overall examination. Interestingly, along with the dreaded directed writing, the translation is the area where students often under perform at prelims but tend to improve on significantly over the last two to three months of the course.

There are reasons for this. Translation is the purest form of testing your comprehension or reading skills, and as these mature over the final stages of the French Higher course, it stands to reason that your translation can improve. I say *can* improve, of course, because there are specific techniques to master before your translating *will* actually get better.

Let us go over what is required. You are required to translate very accurately the section of the text that has been underlined. Often this is a particularly important part of the passage, which seems to be the central point of the article, but this is not always the case. What is invariably true, however, is that you will be expected to have a *full understanding of the whole passage before you even start the translation,* so you must never try to do the translation until you have entirely finished the comprehension section. (Every year the SQA markers refer to a number of cases where it is clear that candidates have thought better of this advice and have decided to attempt the translation part first, and have shown a serious misunderstanding of the general passage as whole.)

The 5–7 lines you have been asked to translate into English are divided into sense units, with each worth 2 marks, giving a total of 10 for the translation.

Remember, this is an exercise which assesses your ability to work accurately, so inaccuracy will be penalised. This table should clarify the marking approach shown for each sense unit, or part of a sentence.

Category	Mark	Description
Good	2	Essential information and all relevant details are understood and conveyed clearly, with appropriate use of English.
Satisfactory	1	Essential information is conveyed clearly and comprehensibly, although some of the details may be translated in an imprecise or inaccurate manner. The key message is conveyed in spite of inaccuracies and weaknesses in the use of English.
Unsatisfactory	0	The candidate fails to demonstrate sufficient understanding of the essential information and relevant details. Errors may include mistranslation and/or the failure to translate relevant details.

There is both good and bad news in all this. If you translate all that there is accurately, into decent English, you will score the maximum 2 in every section. But the pitfalls are many. In our attempts to cover all the original features of the French, we may produce unnatural or stilted or clumsy English. In trying to write more 'normal' English, with one eye on style and fluency, we might miss out an essential ingredient in the French version. In either case, you're down to 1 point out of 2 right away, each time you do it. Do this twice in any sense unit, and you've earned yourself 0. Now you would be forgiven for thinking you are unlikely to miss out any of the features in the original French, but the SQA are past masters of trickery, and the translation is all about setting you traps and testing your wits.

So, translation pieces tend to be full of those awkward little areas of grammar and phraseology which can make French such a **tricky language**. Let's look at some of them as examples so that you can actually learn the grammatical rule at the same time as identifying them as **common villains of the translation**.

✔ la discipline dans les lycées = discipline in schools (use of le/la/les when talking about something generally – in English we don't use any article)

✔ les Français vivent pour manger = (The) French live in order to eat (with or without the definite article in English)

✔ pour jeunes d'ici, nous n'avons pas grande chose = we do not have much for young people around here

✔ une des conséquences de notre système politique = one of the consequences of our political system (un/une as one)

✔ ils n'ont pas de voiture = they do not have a car (pas de not pas un/une in French for 'not a' in English)

✔ il n'a plus d'argent maintenant = he no longer has any money now (ne… plus = no longer)

✔ les parents n'écoutent jamais leurs enfants = parents never listen to their children (ne… jamais = never)

✔ je ne regrette rien = I do not regret anything; I regret nothing (ne… rien = nothing)

✔ personne ne le fait = no one does it (personne + ne = no one)

✔ il ne parle à personne = he does not talk to anyone; he talks to no one

✔ il faisait n'importe quoi pour gagner = he did anything to win (n'importe quoi = any (old) thing)

✔ lequel as-tu choisi? = which one did you choose?

✔ je mange du pain et du beurre = I eat some bread and butter (du/de la /des translated best by 'some')

✔ tout le monde le disait = everyone was saying it (tout le monde means everyone, not all the world, remember!)

✔ tous les jours j'allais en ville = every day I used to go into town (tous/ toutes = every)

✔ chaque fois que j'y vais, c'est comme ça = every time I go there, that's how it is

✔ chacun entre nous est égoiste = each one of us is selfish/we are all selfish (chacun/chacune = each)

✔ j'y vais tout à l'heure = I am going there at once (y can be translated by there)

✔ il m'a raconté une longue histoire, mais je n'y ai pas fait attention = he told me a long story but I paid no attention to it (y also be translated by it/to it)

✔ il s'est décidé d'en devenir le propriétaire = he decided to become its owner (en as possessive adjective, its)

✔ il faut vraiment faire un effort = you really have to make an effort (il faut refers to people in general, often conveyed by you in English)

✔ je n'aime pas tellement ce milieu = I do not much like this area (ce/cette for this; ces for these)

✔ ses employés l'admirent beaucoup = his/her employees admire him/her greatly (ses = his/her and plural object)

✔ l'éducation des enfants, c'est sa responsabilité = it is his/her responsibility to educate the children (sa = his/her plus singular object)

✔ il se dispute souvent avec son père = he often argues with his father (son = his/her singular object)

✔ on n'oublie pas son enfance = one doesn't forget one's childhood

✔ nos amis en France pensent que… = our friends in France think that… (nos = our plus plural object)

✔ pendant la guerre ils on perdu leur maison = during the war they lost their house (leur = their plus singular object)

✔ son oncle, qui est professeur d'anglais = his/her uncle, who is an English teacher (qui refers to the subject; note: jobs take no article)

✔ la femme que j'aime = the woman (whom/that) I love (que refers to the object)

✔ ce que je n'aime pas, c'est se coucher tard = what I don't like is going to bed late

✔ ce qui est très énervant, c'est quand on n'arrive pas parler = what is/what I find very irritating is when you do not manage to speak

✔ la routine journalière? Je la déteste! = daily routine? I hate it! (using le/la/les to refer to a direct object)

✔ je lui ai écrit il y a un mois = I wrote to him/her a month ago (lui refers to an indirect object, i.e. where in French you would use à – j'ai écrit une lettre à…)

✔ je leur ai dit que non = I told them no (leur refers to an indirect object, to them: j'ai dit non à mes parents)

And of course there are many instances of testing your **tense awareness**:

● je joue au rugby toutes les semaines = I play rugby every week

● je joue du piano depuis sept ans = I have been playing the piano for seven years

● j'avais joué déjà quand il a commencé son match = I had already played when he started his match

● j'ai joué contre l'équipe française = I played against the French team

● je jouais tous les jours après l'école = I used to play every day after school

● je vais jouer demain après-midi = I am going to play tomorrow afternoon

● je compte jouer l'année prochaine = I intend to play next year

● j'espère jouer pour mon lycée = I hope to play for my high school

- je ne veux pas jouer si régulièrement = I do not want to play so regularly
- je voudrais jouer de la clarinette = I would like to play the clarinet
- j'aimerais jouer de la guitare aussi = I would also like to play the guitar
- je jouerai quand j'aurai 18 ans = I will play when I am 18 (note double future in the French)
- je jouerais, si tu le voulais = I would play if you wanted (me to) (note conditional plus imperfect)

Student activity

Here are a couple of exercises designed to improve your awareness of tenses. Choose five of the above sentences and, keeping the verb, change the details. E.g. Je joue au handball tous les quinze jours.

Next, take another five sentences and give an alternative spelling of the verb. When you return to these alternatives in a week's time, underline the correct verb form.
E.g Je ne veut/<u>veux</u> pas jouer si régulièrement.

Less frequent is the use of a 'mood' tense, known as the subjunctive, but it is as well to have at least heard of it. Here are some common examples of the phrases which take the subjunctive:

- **il faut que** je m'en *aille* = **I have to** go (or: it is necessary…)
- **il est dommage** qu'il *soit* blessé = **it is a shame that** he is injured
- **bien que** ce *soit* défendu = **although** it is forbidden
- **quoique** ce *soit* trop tard = **although** it is too late
- nous le verrons **avant qu'**il *parte* = we will see him **before** he leaves
- il a brulé la lettre **afin que** personne ne la lise = he burned the letter **so that** no one may read it
- **pourvu qu'**il *soit* content = **provided that** he is happy (avoid misuse of 'providing')
- nous restons ici **en attendant qu'**il *vienne* = we will stay here **till** he comes
- **sans que** vous le *sachiez* = **without** your knowing it
- cela ne m'étonnerait pas qu'il *ait* des problèmes = it would not surprise me that he had problems

But however long the warning list of tricky language, awkward tense work and so on, your main responsibility is to bear in mind the principles of good translation and remember the dos and the don'ts:

Dos

✔ Leave yourself at least 10 minutes out of the 55 for the translation part of Paper I!

✔ Make sure you have answered all the comprehension questions fully before attempting the translation.

✔ Get a grip of the tense(s), and be aware of any tense changes.

✔ Check if there are any words given more than one translation in the dictionary. The bigger the dictionary, the more information on this you are likely to get!

✔ Read the translation lines over and over and over again before starting to translate at all – it is no good to start translating the first line when you don't understand what follows!

✔ Try to divide up the translation lines into what you imagine would be the 'sense units' that the markers will refer to.

✔ In each sense unit, and in each sentence, check that every detail and word in the French has been covered in your translation

✔ Now check that your English makes sense and reads normally.

Don'ts

✗ Never rush into translating straightaway and think that difficulties will iron themselves out in the writing.

✗ Never ever leave blanks, either in the hope of returning to these at the end or just out of cluelessness.

✗ Do not add to what was there – just translate what the author said.

✗ Avoid giving any alternatives or either-ors. (You will always be penalised for this.)

✗ Do not ignore your comprehension of the article so far – this should stand you in good stead for the translation piece.

✗ Do not allow your translation time to spread into your directed writing time!

It would be useful at this stage to have a look at the 2008 translation part of paper I, and to examine how the marking scheme applies what we have discussed so far.

They probably chose the introduction to the passage because it is an opening to the story of short-lived fame and because it is potentially difficult and possibly even confusing. For a start, many of us will not even have heard of Andy Warhol, the celebrated and *celebrity* modern artist.

Secondly, this article is not about him, or indeed, art.

Thirdly, we have a mix of tenses and time zones, moving from past to present to future. That said a good candidate is expected to score at least 8/10 here. Let's see how.

The SQA examiners broke up the paragraph into five sense units:

1) C'est Andy Warhol qui le disait…
2) …à l'avenir, chacun aura son quart d'heure de célébrité.
3) Moi, je suis célèbre depuis plus de quatre mois.
4) Et qu'ai-je fait pour mériter cette renommée?
5) J'ai tout simplement ouvert mon blog sur Internet.

SENSE UNIT 1

Text	Good 2 points	Satisfactory 1 point	Unsatisfactory 0 points
C'est Andy Warhol	It is/was Andy Warhol		Omission of c'est translation
qui	who/that		
le disait	said (it)/used to say (it) would say/said that/this	was saying once said had said	says/was to say

SENSE UNIT 2

Text	Good 2 points	Satisfactory 1 point	Unsatisfactory 0 points
à l'avenir	In (the) future		From now on
chacun	everyone/every body each (and every) person each (one) of us	each	people
aura	will have	would have will become will be will have had	has

son quart d'heure	his/her/their quarter of an hour 15 minutes	a/one's omission of *son* adding his/her <u>own</u>	four hours (*quatre* instead of *quart*) his/her moment a little
de célébrité.	of fame/celebrity/ stardom of being famous	as <u>a</u> celebrity	to celebrate of being celebrated

SENSE UNIT 3

Text	Good 2 points	Satisfactory 1 point	Unsatisfactory 0 points
Moi	Personally Omission of *Moi* (seen as redundant) Me/As for me I myself	However, I... Myself, I... For me... Me myself...	
je suis (depuis)	I have been	I am I have had (fame)	I was I am (since)
célèbre	famous	a celebrity	celebrated
depuis plus de quatre mois.	for more than four months for over four months	<u>since</u> more than four months	since I was four years old a quarter of a month four months ago after more than four months for the past four months (omission of more than)

SENSE UNIT 4

Text	Good 2 points	Satisfactory 1 point	Unsatisfactory 0 points
Et	And	Omission of *et*	
qu'ai-je fait	what have I done what did I do what was it that I did	<u>for</u> what have I done	
pour mériter	(in order) to deserve/merit/earn that deserves	achieve/receive	
cette renommé?	this/that/such/fame/ renown this renowned status this celebrity status	being this celebrated/ renowned my fame reputation/recognition renowned fame status omission of *cette* this celebrity	this (omission of *renommée*) this renownment/ name/celebration/ achievement

SENSE UNIT 5

Text	Good 2 points	Satisfactory 1 point	Unsatisfactory 0 points
J'ai ouvert	I (have) opened (up)/ created/started/set up	I <u>had</u> opened/released/ put/posted/published	I open (present tense)
tout simplement	(quite/just/very) simply simply just	so simply only	<u>all</u> simply <u>all too</u> simply
mon blog	my blog	my <u>own</u> blog <u>a</u> blog	
sur internet.	on the Internet my online blog my Internet blog	<u>on</u> Internet <u>over</u> the Internet <u>to</u> the Internet	

Here is how a good translation of the paragraph might read (without alternatives):

 It was Andy Warhol who said: 'In the future, everyone will have his 15 minutes of fame'. I have been famous for more than four months. And what have I done to deserve this fame? I have simply opened my blog on the Internet.

10/10

3 Directed Writing

Part 1: General

Part 2: Specific

PART 1: GENERAL

The directed writing is section 2 of paper I, but really has nothing to do with the reading comprehension and translation at all. It tests a completely different skill – your ability to carry out instructions and express yourself within a given scenario on paper – and should be treated as a separate part of the French Higher examination altogether.

Time to recall the basics of the directed writing.

- This part of paper I lasts 45 minutes.
- You are to write 150–180 words in French.
- You are given a scenario in English, which typically refers to an experience you are supposed to have had in France, and you are required to write an account of this.
- Your written account has to include the six bullet points given.

PART 2: SPECIFIC

The directed writing tasks are quite predictable, and therefore you are expected to be well prepared – in fact, this part of the exam tests above all your ability to produce rehearsed French. A look over the directed writing tasks from 2001 to 2008 reveals how little they vary and, as a consequence, the extent to which the actual bullet points remain similar.

2001

Last summer, you were asked to represent your school/college at an international youth conference in France.

Now you have been asked to write an account of your experiences **in French** for inclusion in the foreign language section of your school/college magazine.

You must include the following information and **you should try to add** other relevant details:

- where exactly you went and how you travelled
- where you stayed and what you thought of the accommodation
- how you spent your time
- your impression of the people you met
- what you found most interesting about your trip
- how you think your experiences will help you in the future

2002

Your school/college has established links and an exchange programme with a school/college in France. You were sent as part of a group to visit the French school/college.

On your return, you have been asked to write **in French** an account of your experiences for inclusion in the foreign language section of your school/college magazine.

You must include the following information and **you should try to add** other relevant details:

- how you travelled and where you stayed
- where the school/college was situated and what the area was like
- what your impressions were of the school/college
- what excursions were organised for your group
- how you intend to continue the links with the French school/college

2003

Last summer you were invited to the wedding of your pen friend's sister in France.

On your return, you have been asked to write **in French** an account of your experiences for inclusion in the foreign language section of your school/college magazine.

You must include the following information and **you should try to add** other relevant details:

- where exactly you stayed and for how long
- how you travelled and what the journey was like
- what you thought of the area
- what you did on the day of the wedding
- your impressions of the people you met at the wedding
- what you enjoyed most about your visit

2004

Last year you went with a group from your school/college to take part in a sporting event in France organised by your partner school/college.

Now you have been asked to write an account of your experiences **in French** for inclusion in the foreign language section of your school/college magazine.

You must include the following information and **you should try to add** other relevant details:

- where exactly you went and how long you spent there
- who you went with, and what the journey was like
- some details about the people that you met in France, and what you did together
- some information about the sporting event that you took part in
- what aspects of French life you particularly enjoyed
- how you think your experiences will help you in the future

2005

Your area is twinned with a partner town in France. You and a group from your school/college have been selected to be part of an exchange visit to the French town.

On your return from the visit, you have been asked to write an account of your experiences **in French** for inclusion in the foreign language section of your school/college magazine.

You must include the following information and **you should try to add** other relevant details:

- when you went and where you stayed
- who travelled with you and what the journey was like
- what was organised for you as part of the visit
- how you spent your free time
- what you liked and/or disliked about the visit
- how you think the exchange will benefit you and your school/college

2006

Last summer you travelled on your own to the University of Lyon to attend a summer school for young people studying French. While you were there you stayed in the university residence, attended classes during the day and had free time in the evenings.

On your return from the visit, you have been asked to write an account of your experiences **in French** for inclusion in the foreign language section of your school/college magazine.

You must include the following information and **you should try to add** further relevant details:

- how you travelled and why you chose that method of transport
- what the accommodation was like and what you did for meals
- how you spent a typical day
- how you got on with the other students
- how you felt about being away from home on your own
- how you plan to keep in touch with the friends you made.

2007

Your town is twinned with a town in France. Last year you went as part of a group to join in the celebration to mark the twentieth anniversary of the twinning. You stayed with your partner's family.

On your return from the visit you have been asked to write a report **in French** for the foreign language section of your school magazine.

You must include the following information and you should try to add other
relevant details:

- how you travelled and who you went with
- where you stayed and what the accommodation was like
- how you got on with your partner and his/her family
- how the town celebrated the anniversary
- what you did on the last evening
- why you would or would not recommend a stay in a French family to other
  pupils in your school

2008
Last summer you and a group of fellow students went on a study trip to your
twin town, to find out more about it.

On your return from the French visit, you have been asked to write an account
of your experiences **in French** for inclusion in the foreign language section of
your school/college magazine.

You must include the following information and you should try to add other
relevant details:

- where your twin town is **and** whether you had visited it before
- where you stayed **and** what you thought of the accommodation
- what you did during your stay to find out more about the town
- what you liked **or** what you disliked about the town
- what you thought of the people you met during your stay
- how other students in your school/college will benefit from your visit

It should be noted that, since 2004, the following warning has been written at
the bottom of the instructions for the directed writing section:

Marks will be deducted for any area of information that is omitted.

This is worth bearing in mind because although the SQA has always emphasised
the need to include all bullet points, and all elements within a bullet point,
many candidates simply try to avoid the trickier information by leaving it out.
This is the surest way to fail your directed writing.

The bullet points themselves tend to follow a pattern:

Points 1 and 2 set the scene with details of where you went, how you travelled, where you stayed, what you thought of the journey or accommodation, and how many were in the group.

Points 3 and 4 usually concentrate on the purpose of the visit itself, what you did, and what your impressions were of the the people or the experience.

Points 5 and 6 often ask for your reaction to the visit, the good and the bad aspects of the visit, what you feel you have gained from the stay in France, and future contact with people you met, or even recommendations to others in your school or town concerning their involvement in something similar.

In order to gain 15/15 you need to cover all elements of all six bullet points, address these in a clear, structured and balanced manner (giving equal weighting to each one) and continue to observe (as you did in the oral assessment) the absolute need for accuracy and range of language. Finally, it is easy to ignore the instruction given in bold each year that **you should try to add other relevant details,** in other words flesh out the bones of the details so that your writing reads and flows as a proper account of lived experiences in mature French, rather than a list of bullet points. The word count, remember, is to be between 150 and 180.

This seems like the appropriate time to take a closer look at the requirements for a satisfactory or 9/15 versus a very good or 15/15 performance in the directed writing.

The French Higher markers are reminded each year to apply the following criteria to candidates' scripts in the examination.

Satisfactory

Category	Mark	Content	Accuracy	Language resource – variety, range, structures
Satisfactory	9	• The candidate uses mainly simple, more basic sentences • The language is perhaps repetitive and uses a limited range of verbs and fixed phrases not appropriate to this level. • In some examples, one or two bullet points may be less fully addressed. • In some cases, the content may be similar to that of good or very good examples, but with some serious accuracy issues.	• The verbs are generally correct, but basic. • Tenses may be inconsistent, with present tenses being used at times instead of past tenses. • There are quite a few errors in other parts of speech – personal pronouns, gender of nouns, adjective endings, cases, singular/plural confusion – and in the use of accents. • Some prepositions may be inaccurate or omitted, e.g. I went the town. • While the language may be reasonably accurate in 3 or 4 bullet points, in the remaining 2 control of the language structure may deteriorate significantly. • Overall, there is more correct than incorrect and there is the impression overall that the candidate can handle tenses.	• The candidate copes with the past tense of some verbs. • A limited range of verbs is used to address some of the bullet points. • Candidate relies on a limited range of vocabulary and structures. • When using the perfect tense, the past participle is incorrect or the auxiliary verb is omitted on occasion. • Sentences may be basic and mainly brief. • There is minimal use of adjectives, probably mainly after 'is', e.g. 'The boss was helpful'. • The candidate has a weak knowledge of plurals. • There may be several spelling errors, e.g. reversal of vowel combinations.

Very good

Category	Mark	Content	Accuracy	Language resource – variety, range, structures
Very Good	15	• All bullet points are covered fully, in a balanced way, including a number of complex sentences. • Some candidates may also provide additional information. • A wide range of verbs/verb forms, tenses and construction is used. • Overall this comes over as a competent, well thought-out account of the event which reads naturally.	• The candidate handles all aspects of grammar and spelling accurately, although the language may contain some minor errors or even one more serious error. • Where the candidate attempts to use language more appropriate to post-Higher, a slightly higher number of inaccuracies need not detract from the overall very good impression.	• The candidate is comfortable with almost all the language used and generally uses a different verb or verb form in each sentence. • There is good use of a variety of tenses, adjectives, adverbs and prepositional phrases and, where appropriate, word order. • The candidate uses co-ordinating conjunctions and subordinate clauses throughout the writing. • The language flows well.

Just as with the oral assessment, the system of pegged marking is used here, so that your performance will be fitted into one of the six categories:

Very good	15
Good	12
Satisfactory	9
Unsatisfactory	6
Poor	3
Very poor	0

Other than the essential aspects previously mentioned, the criteria grids underline the supreme importance of the **candidate's ability to use tenses accurately,** and this is the defining factor in whether a performance belongs to one of the top three or one of the bottom three categories.

For an extremely useful and more in-depth approach to this, read the section in Leckie and Leckie's *Higher French Course Notes*, pages 58–76. My own students have benefited from this chapter for years, and most of their revision for directed writing centres on these notes.

When and where you went and for how long

Time phrases (past)

- l'année dernière – last year
- l'an dernier – last year
- pendant les grandes vacances – during the summer holidays
- pendant les vacances de Pâques/Noël/été – during the Easter/Christmas/ summer holidays
- l'été dernier – last summer
- il y a quelques mois – a few months ago
- en été/automne/hiver – in the summer/autumn/winter
- au printemps – in the spring
- au mois de juillet – in the month of July

- au début de septembre – at the beginning of September
- à la fin d'août – at the end of August
- pendant le trimestre scolaire – in term-time

Time phrases (future)

- dans le futur – in the future
- à l'avenir – in the future
- après mes examens – after my exams
- après avoir passé mes examens – after having sat my exams
- quand j'aurai 18 ans – when I am 18
- lorsque je serai étudiant(e) à l'université – when I am a university student
- dans quelques mois/années – in a few months'/years' time

I went/We went, and for how long

- je suis allé – I went (masculine)
- je suis allée – I went (feminine)
- on est allé – we went
- nous sommes allés pour quelques jours – we went for a few days
- j'ai passé deux semaines extraordinaires – I spent two amazing weeks
- nous avons passé une quinzaine inoubliable – we spent a memorable fortnight

Where you went

- en France – in France/to France
- dans le nord de la France – in/to the north of France
- à Paris/Lyon – in/to Paris/Lyons
- à Grenoble qui se trouve dans les Alpes près de la Suisse – in/to Grenoble which is situated in the Alps near Switzerland
- à St-Tropez qui est une jolie station balnéaire sur la côte méditerranéenne – in/to St Tropez which is a nice seaside resort on the Mediterranean coast
- à Gornac qui est un joli petit village dans l'ouest de la France à une centaine de kilomètres de Bordeaux – in/to Gornac which is a nice little village in the west of France about a hundred kilometres from Bordeaux

Student activity

Create a grid to test your accuracy with phrases from each heading that you have learned, e.g.

Phrase type	English	French (complete this section)
• Time phrase	During the summer holidays	
• Past verb	We spent a fortnight	
• Where...	In Grenoble not far from the Alps	
etc.		

Who you went with

- C'était un voyage d'études – it was a school trip
- j'ai participé à un échange scolaire – I took part in a school exchange
- il y avait une trentaine d'élèves dans le groupe – there were about 30 pupils in the group
- nous étions à peu près vingt élèves et trois professeurs – we were about 20 pupils and three teachers
- je suis allé(e) avec ma famille, c'est-à-dire ma mère, mon père et ma soeur aînée – I went with my family, that is my mother, my father and my elder sister
- je suis parti(e) avec mes amis du lycée – I went with my school friends
- je suis allé tout seul – I went on my own (masculine)
- je suis allée toute seule – I went on my own (feminine)

How you travelled and what you thought of the trip

Transport

- nous avons pris le train/l'avion/le ferry – we took the train/plane/ferry
- on a voyagé en train/en avion/en car – we travelled by train/plane/coach
- nous avons tout d'abord pris le car de Hawick à Hull, puis nous pris le ferry et ensuite nous avons voyagé en train de Calais à Paris – first of all we took the coach from Hawick to Hull, then took the ferry, and then travelled by train from Calais to Paris

- on est partis en train d'Edimbourg très tôt le samedi matin et on est arrivés tard le dimanche soir à Strasbourg – we left Edinburgh by train very early on Saturday morning and arrived in Strasbourg late on Sunday evening
- nous avons quitté Aberdeen le vendredi matin à bord d'un avion qui nous a amenés jusqu'à Montpellier – we left Aberdeen by plane on the Friday morning which took us to Montpellier
- nous sommes arrivés à Nîmes vers minuit – we arrived at Nimes around midnight

Opinions of the trip

- le voyage était assez long et inconfortable – the journey was quite long and uncomfortable
- plusieurs élèves étaient malades pendant la traversée – quite a few pupils were ill on the crossing
- le voyage a passé très vite parce que j'ai lu mon roman policier et j'ai pu dormir un peu aussi – the journey went quickly because I read my crime novel and was also able to sleep a little
- pour passer le temps, nous avons regardé un bon film d'aventure qui était passionnant – in order to pass the time, we watched a good adventure film which was exciting
- j'ai trouvé le voyage en France un peu ennuyeux mais supportable – I found the journey to France a bit boring but bearable

Where you stayed and what you thought of the accommodation

Accommodation

- nous sommes restés dans une auberge de jeunesse pas loin du centre-ville – we stayed in a youth hostel not far from the town centre
- le camping se trouvait à dix minutes de la plage – the camping was ten minutes from the beach
- on a logé dans un gîte à la campagne – we stayed in a self-catering place in the country
- l'hôtel était dans la banlieue – the hotel was in the outskirts
- la maison de mon correspondant/ma correspondante était située au centre d'une station de ski – my correspondent's house was in the middle of a ski resort

Opinions

- ce qui était commode – which was convenient
- l'hôtel était vieux et charmant, mais sale et peu confortable – the hotel was old and charming, but dirty and not very comfortable
- d'un côté, le logement était moderne et bien décoré, mais de l'autre côté c'était incroyablement laid et sans caractère – on the one hand, the accommodation was modern and well decorated, but on the other hand it was incredibly ugly and characterless
- j'ai dû partager ma chambre, ce qui était un peu gênant – I had to share my room, which was a bit awkward
- j'avais ma propre chambre – j'avais de la chance! – I had my own room – what a stroke of luck!

Information and opinions about the school

- j'ai trouvé que le système scolaire était tout à fait différent – I found that the school system was completely different
- la journée scolaire n'était pas comme chez nous – the school day was not like ours
- ...par exemple, les cours commençaient à huit heures du matin et finissaient à cinq heures de l'après-midi –...for instance, lessons started at 8 a.m. and finished at 5 p.m.
- nous avions une pause de deux heures pour le déjeuner – we had a break of two hours for lunch
- il y avait presque trente-cinq élèves dans la classe d'anglais et ils ne faisaient que de la grammaire! – there were nearly 35 pupils in the English class and they did nothing but grammar!
- le lycée était un vieux bâtiment à quatre étages – the school was an old building on four floors

Information and opinions about the town/area

Town

- la grande ville était animée avec beaucoup de cafés et de restaurants où on mangeait le soir – the city was lively with lots of cafes and restaurants where we would eat in the evening
- le petit village était charmant mais il n'y avait pas grand-chose pour les jeunes, surtout la nuit – the little village was charming but didn't have much for young people, especially at night

- c'était une ville industrielle avec des tours d'habitation et donc un peu laid – it was an industrial town with high-rise buildings and therefore quite ugly
- il y avait pas mal de grands magasins en ville où j'ai acheté des souvenirs pour ma famille – there were quite few department stores where I bought some souvenirs for my family

Area

- la Normandie est une région avec une longue histoire intéressante avec ses musées, ses monuments historiques, ses châteaux et ses traditions – Normandy is a region with a long and interesting history, with its museums, historic monuments, castles and traditions
- j'ai vraiment apprécié la beauté de cette région, avec ses forêts, ses montagnes et ses lacs – I really appreciated the beauty of this region, with its forests, mountains and lakes
- d'une part, il y avait de belles vues à admirer ici, mais d'autre part je trouvais qu'il y avait peu pour les touristes – on the one hand, you could admire the beautiful views here, but yet again there was little for tourists

Information about the job and responsibilities/duties

- j'ai travaillé comme barman/serveur/serveuse – I worked as a barman/waiter/ waitress
- j'ai travaillé comme réceptionniste – I worked as a receptionist
- j'étais femme de chambre dans un hôtel – I was a chambermaid in a hotel
- je devais prendre les commandes et servir les clients – I had to take orders and serve customers
- j'étais responsable du service des tables – I was responsible for table service
- je devais répondre au téléphone et prendre les réservations – I had to answer the phone and take bookings
- je devais accueillir les clients – I had to welcome the guests
- il fallait nettoyer les chambres tous les jours – I had to clean the rooms every day

What you thought of the people

Positives

- tout le monde était très accueillant – everyone was very welcoming
- je me suis bien amusé avec mon correspondant, qui avait heureusement les mêmes intérêts que moi – I had a good time with my pen friend (masculine), who fortunately had the same interests as me

- je me suis amusée avec ma correspondante, qui était sportive et bavarde comme moi – I had a good time with my pen friend (feminine), who was sporty and chatty like I am
- on avait les mêmes goûts – we had the same tastes
- j'ai beaucoup aimé ma famille, qui m'a vraiment gâté(e) – I liked my family a lot, they really spoiled me
- je me suis bien entendu(e) avec tout le monde – I got on well with everyone
- les profs et les élèves français étaient tellement heureux de nous recevoir – the French teachers and pupils were so happy to have us

Negatives

- il faut dire que je ne m'entendais pas bien avec mon correspondant/ma famille/les élèves – I have to say I did not get on well with my pen friend/family/the pupils
- je le trouvais difficile de parler aux autres et de les comprendre – I found it hard to talk to the others and to understand them
- mon patron était affreux – my boss (masculine) was awful
- …il criait tout le temps –…he shouted all the time
- ma patronne était affreuse – my boss (feminine) was awful
- …elle ne parlait à personne –…she didn't speak to anyone

What there was to do (in my free time)

One-offs (on a single occasion, so using perfect tense)

- le premier jour, on est allé voir les monuments historiques – on the first day, we went to see the historic monuments
- une fois, on s'est promené dans le vieux quartier de la ville – one time, we went for a walk in the old town
- nous avons fait du shopping et j'ai acheté des cadeaux pour mes amis – we went shopping and I bought presents for my friends
- nous avons fait beaucoup d'activités aquatiques – par exemple, j'ai fait de la planche à voile, de la plongée sous-marine, du surf et de la voile – we did lots of water sports – for example, I went wind-surfing, deep-sea diving, surfing and sailing
- un soir, on a mangé la spécialité régionale dans un restaurant – one evening we ate the local dish in a restaurant

Repeated actions or descriptions (imperfect tense)

- on faisait tous les jours une petite excursion – every day we went on a short outing
- après le travail on se baignait et ensuite on sortait en ville pour quelque chose à manger – after work we would go for a swim and then go out for something to eat
- il y avait tant de choses à faire: on pouvait faire du ski, du patinage, de l'escalade – there was so much to do: you could go skiing, skating, climbing
- la station offrait beaucoup à faire la nuit, car la vie nocturne était vraiment animée – the resort offered lots to do at night, because the night life was lively
- de temps en temps, on faisait du lèche-vitrines, car les magasins étaient tellement chers – now and again we used to go window shopping, since the shops were so expensive
- on mangeait dans de bons restaurants français qui n'étaient pas si chers que chez nous – we ate in good French restaurants which were not as dear as with us
- on se levait tôt et se couchait tôt – la routine journalière était vraiment fatigante – we got up early and went to bed early – the daily routine was really tiring!

What you thought of the trip/whole experience

Positives

- ce qui m'a surtout émerveillé, c'était la gentillesse – what really amazed me was the kindness
- ce que j'ai aimé le plus, c'était la nourriture française – what I liked the best was the French food
- j'ai absolument adoré ma famille – I simply loved my family
- il a fait super beau pendant tout mon séjour – c'était extra! – the weather was fantastic during my whole stay – it was brilliant!
- quelle expérience inoubliable! – what an unforgettable experience!
- je me suis vraiment amusé(e) pendant ce voyage – I really enjoyed myself on this trip
- à mon avis, la ville d'Avignon était sensationnelle – in my opinion, the town of Avignon was sensational
- j'ai beaucoup amélioré mon français – my French really improved
- c'est un voyage que je n'oublierai jamais – it's a trip I'll never forget

Negatives

- malheureusement, je n'ai pas aimé la ville/la région où j'étais – unfortunately, I didn't like the town/region where I was
- il n'y avait pas grand-chose à faire ni à voir – there wasn't much to do or see
- je m'ennuyais à mourir – I was bored to death
- le logement était sale et ma chambre trop petite – the accommodation was dirty and my room too small
- la nourriture était affreuse – the food was terrible
- je n'ai pas pu supporter mon corres/patron – I couldn't stand my pen friend/boss
- je n'ai pas perfectionné mon français – I didn't improve my French
- je n'ai pas eu l'occasion de parler en français – I didn't have the chance to speak in French

Notes on the future/recommendations

- j'aimerais y retourner un jour – I would to return there one day
- j'aimerais beaucoup refaire un voyage semblable dans le futur – I would like to do a similar trip again in the future
- je suis d'avis que ce serait une bonne expérience pour tous les élèves de mon âge – I am of the opinion that it would be a good experience for all pupils of my age
- je dirais que voir un autre pays et rencontrer des gens de différentes culture vaudrait la peine – I would say that seeing another country and meeting people of different cultures would be worthwhile
- je crois que c'est un bon moyen d'apprendre la langue – I believe it's a good way to learn the language
- mais attention – cela ne serait pas si facile que ça! – But be careful – it would not be as easy as all that!

You can see, therefore, that there is plenty of learning preparation to be done for this part of paper I – any time spent learning the above phrases, whether exactly as they are here or with your own changes made to them, would be time well spent.

 Remember that anything you learn for the directed writing will of course be useful for your short essay which follows the listening comprehension in paper II!

Finally, before going on to look at a satisfactory and a very good directed writing, we should focus on a few timely dos and don'ts:

Dos

✔ *Plan the essay in paragraphs.*

✔ *Ensure all bullet points are fully communicated.*

✔ *Stick to the French you know.*

✔ *Add details of your own.*

✔ *Add more than the 'bare minimum' French – time phrases, discursive expressions, opinions, reflections, etc.– i.e. show the level of your competence!*

✔ *Take extra care with your tense endings.*

✔ *Play safe.*

Don'ts

✗ *Translate from the English bullet points.*

✗ *Write in bullet point formation.*

✗ *Start writing French you've never written before.*

✗ *Mix tenses, e.g. La nourriture était affreuse – je déteste ça!*

Directed writing 2008: satisfactory performance

Before reading this through, you should consult the details of the 2008 paper (see page 51), in order to familiarise yourself with the scenario and bullet points. All errors are underlined here, as they are in other exemplar answers later on in this book.

 L'année <u>dernier</u> je suis allé en France avec mon <u>ecole</u>. La ville en France s'appelle Bailleul. Bailleul est notre ville jumelle. <u>Je n'ai pas visité</u> Bailleul quand <u>jétais</u> petit.

Nous sommes restés dans les familles. Ma famille était <u>trés</u> sympa et bonne et la maison était <u>trés</u> grande.

J'ai <u>visitée</u> le centre ville, c'était ennuyeux. Les magasins <u>étaienet</u> petits et pas <u>trés</u> intéressants. J'ai aimé le restaurant, j'ai mangé une baguette avec <u>fromage et jambon!</u> Le samedi, on a rencontré les élèves au collège et j'ai parlé en français! Tout le monde a parlé!

J'ai vu les monuments historiques avec le groupe et mon <u>professuer</u>. Après on a acheté des souvenirs (un t-shirt pour mon ami Gerry). J'ai acheté un <u>cadeaux</u>

pour la famille <u>en</u> Bailleul, ils sont sympa. Le musée était intéressant parce que j'aime <u>l'histiore.</u>

Mon partenaire s'appelle Gérard il est grand et sportif et gentil. Il joue au volley tous les jours. Je <u>n'ai</u> pas sportif je déteste le volleyball, le basketball, le cricket. La <u>méré</u> était aimable et elle a donné <u>moi</u> un livre de Bailleul.

En <u>générale</u>, le voyage était bon et c'est une très bonne idée pour vous. Je retournerai l'année prochaine après mes <u>exams</u> pour deux semaines!

(218 words)

Analysis

This essay communicates the essential details outlined in the bullet points adequately and manages to retain a general grip on tenses – but no more than just satisfactorily.

Firstly, let us examine the bullet points.

Bullet point	Coverage	Evaluation
• where your twin town is and whether you had visited it before	– in France – did not visit it when younger	– satisfactory
• where you stayed and what you thought of the accommodation	– with a family – big house	– satisfactory, but short on opinion
• what you did during your stay to find out more about the town	– visited town centre, shops – ate out at restaurants – met pupils in school on Saturday – historical sites – bought souvenirs/present – museum visit	– satisfactory in one sense, i.e. these experiences obviously made him find out more about the town, but ... – unsatisfactory in the sense that there is no reference to any kind of investigation or research into the town
• what you liked or disliked about the town	– opinions expressed about town centre, shops, restaurant, museum	– satisfactory
• what you thought of the people you met during your stay	– opinions expressed about host mother and partner	– satisfactory/unsatisfactory, giving minimal information and showing barely adequate reflection

Bullet point	Coverage	Evaluation
• how other students in your school/college will benefit from your visit	– mention that such a visit would be good 'for you' (pour vous?)	– unsatisfactory/poor – no real attempt to fulfil requirement of bullet point to say how/why it will benefit the school

With the bullet point analysis out of the way, our next area of focus is the quality of language itself, and principal among language features is the use of tenses. In the response above these are generally sound – more than satisfactory, in fact. Firstly, the present tense, when used to describe the twin town of Bailleul and then his partner Gérard and his 'host' mother, is accurate, if basic (mostly *être* and *avoir*). The perfect (or passé composé) is an area of relative success in the writing, as it is almost all correct, with not only a variety of (10) past participles (both regular and irregular, and verbs conjugated with *avoir* and *être*), but also of subject pronouns (*je/on/nous*).

The imperfect tense is used, more or less accurately, in the appropriate situations when discussing how things were/used to be. This shows an awareness of the important distinction between perfect and imperfect. Finally, the single instance of the proper future tense (*je retournerai*) allows an attempt at the final bullet point (although this candidate has missed the point about what he was meant to say here), where a weaker pupil might not have made such an attempt. There is certainly *'the overall impression that the candidate can handle tenses'* (as is required in the marking criteria above).

In other areas of the language there is evidence of a generally satisfactory directed writing essay. The majority of the information requested has been given, but the writing is not purely data base. The opinions offered are very basic, but the use of adjectives at least allows the candidate to express his views on the town centre, the shops, the museum, the partner and his family, and to reflect on his experience abroad. The sentence structure is adequate, and the overall organisation of the piece, with an effort to divide itself into paragraphs, is definitely of a pass standard.

However, there are sufficient weaknesses to ensure that this performance could not gain any higher a mark than 9/15. There are some notable examples of poor tense use (*j'ai visitée* and *les magasins étaienet petits*) and difficulty with the indirect object produces the clumsy *elle a donné moi un livre* (instead of *elle m'a donné un livre*).

And although we have argued that there is sufficient evidence to suggest a satisfactory standard of descriptive language, the adjectives are very basic (*petit/*

grand/sportif/gentil/bon, etc.), and below the expected Higher standard. The misspelling of straightforward vocabulary is a feature that does not dominate the piece but still regularly appears: *un cadeaux; mon professuer; en générale; mes exams.*

However, probably the most telling aspect of the writing is the need to keep to short, easy sentences and the limited nature of the sentence structure. (Half of the sentences, for example, are under ten words in length.)

Very good performance

 L'été dernier, je suis allée à Nîmes, dans le sud de la France, avec un groupe scolaire afin d'étudier la région. C'était ma première visite là-bas et j'ai trouvé l'expérience très intéressante.

Nous avons logé dans une auberge de jeunesse au centre-ville, ce qui était bien commode, mais un peu bruyant. Nous étions tous dans un grand dortoir au deuxième étage – c'était un groupe de huit garçons. Le père aubergiste était vraiment sympa et il a parlé en anglais pour être aimable.

Tous les jours on sortait en ville pour mieux connaître Nîmes et ses alentours. On a fait des interviews pour notre reportage pour l'école. En plus, on a fait un tour de la région en car, ce qui était utile.

A mon avis, cette vieille ville était très belle avec beaucoup de monuments historiques. Pourtant, de l'autre côté, c'était aussi sale et pollué, car il y avait trop de voitures. Tout le monde que on a <u>recontré</u> était tellement <u>serviables</u> et nous a aidé.

Quand nous sommes retournés chez nous en Ecosse, nous avons publié notre reportage et les élèves le trouvaient intéressants. J'aimerais y retourner un jour dans le futur pour revoir la région.

(205 words)

Analysis

This is a strong performance where the candidate consistently writes at grade A level, demonstrating very good competence in grammar and range of structures and vocabulary, all accurately employed.

Bullet points

Bullet point	Coverage	Evaluation
• Where your twin town is and whether you had visited it before	– does not state it is twin town – says not visited town before	– good
• Where you stayed and what you thought of your accommodation	– youth hostel … – … convenient in town centre – … but noisy	– very good
• What you did during your stay to find out more about the town	– went out every day into town – did interviews – bus tour	– lots of details
• What you liked or disliked about the town	– old and beautiful … – … but dirty, polluted and too many cars	– lots of details
• What you thought of the people that you met during your stay	– nice and helpful	– good
• How other students in your school/will benefit from your visit	– report in school paper – pupils thought it interesting	– very good

As with the coverage of the bullet points, the quality of language is clearly very good. It reads likes a piece of authentic French, rather than a series of bullet points in a translation exercise into the foreign language – it has the fluency of someone who is in control of the crucial aspects of Higher French.

The tense work is very sound, with an appropriate range. The perfect tense successfully covers a variety of past participles (*allé/logé/parlé/fait/rencontré/aidé/ trouvé/publié/retourné*), *avoir* and *être* verbs, regular and irregular verbs and several subject pronouns (*je/il/on/nous/ils*). The past tense work is well balanced out by the many examples of the imperfect, correctly used to express opinions about the experience (referring to the town, its people, the accommodation, etc.). The piece ends with a future conditional (*j'aimerais y retourner*). There is throughout in the tenses a very high degree of accuracy and control, and the tense work is well supported by time phrases, such as *l'été dernier, tous les jours, le dernier jour, quand (nous sommes retournés)*.

An important feature of this writing is the richness of expression and phraseology: *pour mieux connaître Nîmes; pour revoir la région; en plus…; à mon avis…; pourtant….; de l'autre côté.* Adjectives are strengthened by the adverbs that precede them: the warden was *vraiment sympa*; the position of the hostel was *bien commode* although *un peu bruyant*; the townsfolk were *tellement serviables.* In fact, the descriptive nature of the writing is impressive when we consider the number of (more advanced) adjectives in use (*scolaire/ commode/bruyant/aimable/serviable/utile/pollué*). There are also a few successful attempts at using *ce qui* – which Higher students can find difficult. And the inclusion of nouns such as *père aubergiste, alentours, reportage, dortoir* is more than most candidates will offer in a writing examination. In short, this comes across as a very controlled, accurate, competent and organised directed writing performance.

Of course, there are one or two errors: *on a <u>recontré</u>* (should be *on a <u>rencontré</u>*); *tout le monde était <u>serviables</u>* (should be <u>serviable</u>). It might also be argued that some of the language is not particularly advanced: words such as *sympa, belle, intéressant(e)* are vocabulary from a much earlier stage of language learning. But these points do not detract significantly from the whole, which is generally of a very high standard.

Student activity

Once you have tried a past paper, make a note of vocabulary, phrases and use of tenses. You will need to limit what you write down, focusing on key items only. Take the specimen reading comprehension and translation paper as an example:

Vocabulary	
le vacancier	holiday maker
les sables chauds	the hot sands
se bronzer	to sunbathe
fleuri	in bloom/flower
les stations balnéaires	seaside resorts

Phrases	
Il ne faudrait pas croire	You shouldn't think
D'où la popularité...	Which is the reason for its popularity...
En plus...	Moreover...
Très en vogue aussi,...	What is also very much in fashion, is...
...pour ne pas dire...	...not to mention...

Tense work	
Il a réservé des chambres…	He booked rooms…
Les enfants vont jouer…	The children are going to play…
La France est devenue…	France has become…
Il veut que l'eau de la mer soit claire…	He wants the seawater to be clear…
Elle peut assortir…	She can select/pick and choose…

4 Listening

Part 1: General

Part 2: Listening comprehension

PART 1: GENERAL

Paper II consists of the listening comprehension (section A) and writing (section B), lasting 1 hour and totalling 30 marks. Section A lasts approximately 20 minutes and is marked out of 20 (counting for 20% of the overall Higher examination).

The listening comprehension, involving written answers to questions in English, is a dialogue of 2–3 minutes' duration, played twice, and is related to the prescribed themes and topics found in the Arrangements Documents. The use of a dictionary is permitted at any time. (The important difference between this examination in listening and the NAB is that the latter plays the text three times and does not permit the use of a dictionary and of course the listening NAB is not followed by a short essay in French!)

PART 2: LISTENING COMPREHENSION

Candidates get understandably worried about the listening exam. They feel that there is little or nothing they can do to improve their chances, that it depends on the day, that there is too much going on, too much to write down, that the conversation is too fast and that it is more about speed and co-ordination and multi-tasking than about whether or not they can actually understand spoken French.

And they have a point: when, in a real-life situation, are you expected to listen to a high-level discussion in French, and read and answer comprehension questions on it in English almost simultaneously? But exams are always artificial, and what we need to do is decide how best to prepare our students for this most artificial of situations.

First of all, there is no better time to remind you of the need to build up a large *passive* vocabulary – that is, words that you recognise quickly and whose meaning you readily understand. In your final couple of months before the Higher French exam you should be learning/testing yourself on vocabulary at least twice a week, working your way through topic vocabulary and taking out 10–15 new words or phrases from every reading or listening comprehension or past paper exercise you practise on. Although you are allowed a dictionary in the listening examination, this is meant to give you the opportunity to look up difficult or unusual or new words rather than the standard topic vocabulary from the syllabus.

In other words, you will be expected to know the vast majority of the text you hear. So get organised with your vocabulary learning and revise systematically.

Remember that this also increases your chances of doing well in the reading comprehension exam!

However, there is much more that can be done to improve your chances with this paper, starting with an understanding of what the examiners are looking for. The full extract from the Arrangements Documents will follow but, in short, the listening comprehension assesses your ability to obtain a high proportion of factual information and key details accurately, including

- major points (ideas, points of view, lines of argument)
- minor points (one word answers, singe items of vocabulary).

Grade C	Grade A
Listens to a conversation of some complexity between two speakers in the target language on subjects related to the prescribed themes, and obtains factual information with a *satisfactory level of detail and accuracy.*	Listens to a conversation of some complexity between two speakers in the target language on subjects related to the prescribed themes, and obtains factual information with a ***high level of detail and accuracy.***
Speakers will articulate clearly at reasonable speed.	Speakers will articulate clearly at reasonable speed.

• Extracts and understands **essential information from stimulus material** which contains a number of major and subsidiary points, including the expression of points of view. • Understands a **satisfactory proportion of points of detail** and **some of the opinions/ideas expressed.** • Understands **only partially stimulus material of some complexity.**	• Extracts and understands **key items of information and additional items of detail from stimulus material** which contains a number of major and subsidiary points, including the expression of points of view. • Understands a **high proportion of points of detail** and **grasps opinions/ideas expressed.** • Understands **stimulus material of some complexity.**

As the italics show, the difference between satisfactory and very good candidates is in the *extent of the understanding shown in the answers,* so it is clearly important to learn to *demonstrate your comprehension to the full.*

There will always be questions on the shorter, easier points of detail, which are more or less testing your vocabulary, as well as those on more complex facts or a collection of details.

Every Higher listening text will assess your ability to understand concepts or ideas, and people's opinions of these, so you need at times to stand back from the tiny detail and see the big picture. Many students will not reach a top grade because they have failed to grasp the general impression or the broader canvas.

Recall the advice given to you in the section on translation: it is crucial to show an overall understanding of the main idea or picture, and the same applies here!

The examiners go to some lengths to ask questions which test all these various types of comprehension skills, and when you are practising in class or doing a past paper you ought to be aware that listening is a general term covering many skills.

A very useful exercise is to look over a past paper and examine the different types of questions with the transcript in front of you. When you track down the part of the transcript on which you base your answer, time after time, you should be able to distinguish between the types of language in the original text. This is proof of the complexity of the listening skills required at Higher level.

If we go over the paper II section A listening of recent Higher examinations we begin to see which themes and topics are involved.

2001
Antoine is asking Isabelle for her views on smoking.
This also covers a more diverse discussion of healthy and unhealthy lifestyles, touching on free time, entertainment, life in schools, government campaigns, etc.

2002
Adèle, a young student, talks about her life at Montpellier University.
Other topics included in this exam are: school subjects, personal freedom, the description of a town, student accommodation, part-time jobs.

2003
Tristan talks about his holidays at his grandparents' house in Carolles.
Included in the dialogue is discussion about family relationships and character descriptions, pros and cons of family holidays, rules and freedom, daily routine and household chores.

2004
Marie-Claire is being interviewed about her career in tourism.
This is mostly concerned with the details of Marie-Claire's job, but the variety of her job gives rise to many different aspects of dealing with people; she also talks about her past education and her future plans. (Many candidates panicked in my school when they heard the first recording, but by the end of this part of the paper they realised how broad this listening topic actually was!)

2005
Annick talks to us about her career as an athlete.
We also hear about health, fitness and diet, and in describing her lifestyle in detail, Annick gives information about her daily routine and family.

2006
Madame Fourniret, a school teacher, is talking about her job.
There is a description of the actual school itself, what her job entails, a typical day at work, the pupils, and reference to the wider social problems she uncovers, before discussing the merits of learning a foreign language!

2007
Aurélie, a student in Paris, is discussing life in the capital city.
This is about the good and bad qualities of student life in Paris, with reference to tourists, social issues such as unemployment and poverty, and her aspirations for a future life elsewhere.

2008
Francine is talking about the part-time jobs that she has had.
This is a great excuse to bring in a multitude of experiences – Francine as a waitress, child minder, work colleague, student, daughter – and therefore cuts

across several topics and ideas including work-life balance, money, happiness and relationships with others.

In addition to the kind of 'mapping' exercise above, where we see the types of topics covered over the past eight years, it is also useful to identify the grammar which features in the listening examinations, especially the use of tenses.

Year	Tenses	Other grammar
2001	• present (including two verbs together, *je peux pas résister,* etc.) • perfect (covering the events of first smoking, etc.) • imperfect (describing when Isabelle started to smoke, the circumstances, etc.) • conditional (mixed in with an imperfect *si je pouvais, je ne fumerais plus*)	• difficult question forms (*quand est-ce que tu as commencé…?; qu'est-ce que tu fais donc…?*) • use of direct object pronoun (*ma première cigarette, je l'ai fumé…*) • negatives (use of *jamais…; je ne fumerais plus…*)
2002	• present (describing student life now, Montpellier, etc. Sometimes difficult, as in use of reflexive in **s'habitue très vite**) • perfect (often mixed in with imperfect, as in when she talks of her accommodation, her studies; sometimes difficult, as in *il a fallu…établir des règles, je me suis rendue compte que…*) • imperfect (dominates the passage, since it is a reflective piece on her early experiences as a student, focusing on feelings) • subjunctive (*il a fallu que je trouve…*)	• lots of opinion-based language, with explanations and justifications of why she felt the way she did (*j'ai trouvé difficile de réviser car…*) • plenty of descriptive language (so lots of imperfect!) with adjectives and adverbs
2003	• present (explaining what kind of holidays his parents normally prefer; his routine holidays; relationships with his cousins; household chores, etc.) • two verbs together (*mes parents peuvent partir en vacances…; j'aime mieux rester*) • subjunctive (*ils veulent que j'aie les meilleures notes possibles*) • use of infinitives (*préparer les légumes, aller au marché, choisir des fromages, chercher du pain*, etc)	• changing subjects/subject pronouns (parents, grandparents, cousins, Tristan) • opinions (likes and dislikes of types of holidays, responses to various situations, such as school work, stress of workload, etc.) • use of adjectives to describe holidays, feelings, perspectives on routines of work and housework

Year	Tenses	Other grammar
2004	• present (to describe resort of St-Jacques, Marie-Claire's job, her views of tourists of different nationalities) • perfect (when she started her job as tourist guide, then as tour operator)	• complex question forms, with several details (*Quels sont vos plans pour l'avenir? Souhaitez-vous continuer à faire ce que vous faites actuellement?*)
2005	• present (talking about healthy lifestyles, diet, exercise she normally takes, training routines, leisure time, women's place in sport) • two verbs together (*les ingrédients doivent contenir...; j'aime passer la soirée...; ça doit être régulier...*) • perfect (to talk about achievements so far; women's progress in sport) • imperfect (to describe her training routine when she was younger; how she felt about competitive sport as a youngster; what her mother thought of a sports career for her) • after having done something: *après avoir mangé...* • future anterior (!) (*elle aurait préféré* = she would have preferred) • subjunctive (*elle n'aimait pas...que sa petite fille devienne athlète*) • *il faut* + infinitive (used to talk in general terms about the dos/don'ts for an athlete (*il faut faire attention à ça; il faut se consacrer entièrement...*)	• *Il faut* + nouns (*il faut aussi la concentration mentale; il faut le désir...*) • use of 'impersonal' subject pronouns to emphasise generality (*il faut...* = one needs ...; *si on veut manger sainement...*) • time phrases important here as she reflects on her whole career, and projects to her future (*d'abord/toujours/tous les jours/depuis l'âge de seize ans/quand j'étais encore au lycée/à cinq heures du matin/maintenant*) • points of view, contrasting her own and her mother's – both at the beginning and now (we have to be aware of whose opinion it is and when)
2006	• present (describing her job, school, pupils, and society nowadays; her professional routines; views on languages); some awkward verbs (see opposite) • two verbs together (*on peut manger à la cantine; ils veulent quitter la ville; je peux bavarder; il peuvent toujours trouver quelque chose à faire...*)	• descriptive and opinion-based language is the most important here, as Mme Fourniret reflects on her working life, often comparing and contrasting (*les heures me conviennent; il y en a de toutes sortes; ils ne s'intéressent pas beaucoup à d'autres sont plus ambitieux et travaillent dur*)

2007	• nothing of note!	• use of *me* in *mes parents me paient le logement;…pour m'offrir des vêtements…* • comparative: *les gens sont (…) plus stressés que…* • that which: *ce que je trouve amusant, c'est que…; ce qui est triste, c'est que…(…)*
2008	• perfect (to talk about what she has gained from her jobs; how she has kept in contact with past colleagues) • imperfect (the dominant tense here, as Francine talks about the routines of past jobs, how clients and colleagues were, her parents' views of her jobs at the time). Imperfect tense used in questions (see opposite).	• awkward questions using *aviez-vous* (to find out about what she had/did); also *y avait-il* question (to enquire about what there was/were) • important to keep track of shifting subject pronouns, as Francine talks about experiences/perspectives of her own, of her parents, of clients and of colleagues

If you examine the topics and grammar across the listening exams you should begin to see some clear trends.

- Most passages will centre on a 'core' topic, but will involve other themes and topics too.
- The nature of the conversation is personal and anecdotal, as it discusses how the individual is or has been affected.
- This, in turn, engages the speaker and listener in personalised, discursive, opinion-based language.
- And shifts the perspective from one tense to another.

The rich variety of language used by the main speaker allows the examiner to test you on the following:

- understanding of different question forms in French;

 More time should be spent on these, as they provide the focus of the main text!

- key topic-based vocabulary;
- tense-sensitivity, i.e. your ability to move with the speaker as he/she shifts from past to present to future;

- your understanding of reasons given for points of view, opinions, lines of argument;
- your ability to distinguish between information-based and opinion-based language;
- an awareness of turns of phrase and expressions, where meaning is conveyed through an understanding of the whole sense of a collection of words, rather than by the straightforward translation of vocabulary.

You might feel that the last point suggests something almost unfair about the listening comprehension, as there is no way that Higher students can prepare themselves for the full range of tricky French expressions, but in fact going through the transcripts and picking them out is an incredibly useful exercise.

 This is also excellent practice for the reading comprehension and translation, especially the latter, where it is the sense of the whole or parts of the sentences which prove the hardest to grasp.

The following offers a small but meaningful selection of some of these phrases.

2001

- Je suis trop jeune pour *m'en* inquiéter. (I am too young to worry *myself about it*.)
- On ne sait jamais *ce qui vous attend*. (You never know *what's waiting for you*/round the corner.)
- On *y* voit toujours des élèves qui fument. (You always see pupils smoking *there*.)
- En fin de compte…(In actual fact…)
- Si je pouvais, je *ne* fumerais *plus*. (If I could, I would not smoke *any more*.)

2002

- Pour *m'assurer* une meilleure carrière après. (To *guarantee me* a better job later.)
- Ça *te plaisait* d'être loin de chez toi? (*Did you like/mind* being far from home?)
- On a *fini par s'entendre* très bien. (We *ended up getting on* really well.)
- *Il a fallu* d'abord établir des règles. (Firstly, *we had to* establish a few rules.)
- *Il fallait* nous débrouiller seul. (*We had to* sort it out ourselves.)
- Mais *ça en valait la peine*. (But *it was worth it*.)

2003

- Partir en vacances avec mon père et ma mère *ne me dit plus rien.* (Going on holiday with my father and mother *doesn't interest me any more.*)
- d'ailleurs...(besides...)
- C'est pour ça que...(That's why I...)
- *Il faut* aussi leur dire...(*We also have to* tell them...)
- à part ça...(apart from that...)

2004

- *En quoi consiste* votre travail? (*What does* your job *consist of?*)
- La partie *la plus intéressante* de mon travail. (*The most interesting part* of my job.)
- Il faut absolument *savoir parler*.... (You absolutely have *to know how to speak*...)
- ...*au moins* deux langues étrangères. (...*at least* two foreign languages.)
- Je suis *tout à fait* contente de ma carrière. (I'm *completely* happy with my job.)

2005

- avant tout...(above all...)
- Un futur champion *a besoin de* toutes ces qualités. (A future champion *needs* all of these qualities.)
- A mon avis...(In my opinion...)
- *jusqu'*à *la fin de* mon entraînement (*until* my training session *was over*)
- *Elle aurait préféré* me voir infirmière.... (*She would have preferred* to see me become a nurse...)
- *Quelque chose de* délicieux à manger. (*Something* delicious to eat.)

2006

- Les heures *me conviennent.* (The hours *suit me.*)
- Ça *me permet de* passer une journée en ville. (It *allows me to* spend a day in town.)
- d'habitude...(usually...)
- Je ne *dirais* pa ça. (I *would*n't *say* that.)
- *Quelques-uns* arrivent au collège en car scolaire. (*Some of them* come in on the school bus.)
- ...*d'autres* ont un parent qui les transporte (*others* get a lift from a parent)
- eux...(as for them...)

2007

- (Paris) est animé de jour comme de nuit (Paris is lively day and night.)
- Des cafés où personne ne parle français (Cafés where no one speaks French.)
- Bien sûr que oui! (Of course it is!)
- Il faut absolument que les touristes travaillent (Tourists really have to work.)
- Ce qui est vraiment triste, c'est qu'ils sont tellement nombreux (What is really sad is how many of them there are.)
- Les gens ne font plus attention à eux (People don't pay attention to them anymore.)

2008

- *Aviez-vous* un job à temps partiel? (*Did you have* a part-time job?)
- D'autre part.... (on the other hand...)
- Je m'entendais *plutôt bien* avec eux. (Got on *pretty well* with them.)
- La plupart d'entre eux...(the majority of them...)
- Les études *passent avant tout*...(School work *comes first*...)
- Ils se rappellent *toujours* de moi. (They *still* remember me.)

Student activity

Create your own phrase and vocabulary grid to revise the above language; this will test your ability to translate quickly both ways.

French	English
• Je m'entendais bien avec eux	
	• They still remember me
• Je suis trop jeune pour m'inquiéter	
	• You absolutely have to…
• Les heures me conviennent	

So, we have covered the topics, the grammar and the tricky phrases that make this such an exacting paper.

Time now to have a close look at the most recent listening examination, and concentrate not only on the meaning of what is said but how to demonstrate our understanding, and be aware of the answer techniques required to score full marks at each stage.

2008 Higher French Paper II: Listening / Writing Marking Instructions

 Go to www.leckiepastpapers.co.uk to download the audio file.
Please note that underlinings denote essential information.

1)

a) Francine had two evening jobs. What were they and how often did she do them? **2 points**

Acceptable answers
   – As a waitress/server
   OR
   She worked/works in a restaurant
   PLUS twice a week/two nights/evenings/days a week

Unacceptable answers
   – 3 times a week (wrong number)
   – at the weekend (instead of during the [whole] week)

Acceptable answers
   – As a babysitter/childminder
   OR
   She watched/watches/looks after/takes care of children
   PLUS on Wednesdays/once a week

Unacceptable answers
   – works with/helps children (as opposed to being responsible for them)
   – on Wednesday and at the weekend

NB Each point requires job + when

b) What does Francine say is the advantage of working in the evening? **1 point**

Acceptable answers
   – The pay is better (than during the day)/gets more money/it's not as good pay during the day

Unacceptable answers
   – good pay/it's well paid (without the comparison)
   – has more money (without saying why)
   – double the amount (inaccurate)

NB Must be idea of comparison

2) Why had Francine decided to get a job? **2 points**

Acceptable answer
   – To pay for her shopping (trips)/she likes shopping/loves shops

Unacceptable answer
- her <u>daily</u> shopping
- shopping <u>and</u> magazines

Acceptable answer
- To learn about/discover/experience/know/get used to the world of work/job world/working world/for work experiences

Unacceptable answer
- to get into (a particular line of work)
- to help her in…
- any mention of <u>travel</u> negates the right answer (as it undermines the comprehension)

3) She liked one job better than the other.
   a) Why did she prefer that job?   **2 points**

Acceptable answer
- She could <u>have fun/play</u> with the children

Unacceptable answer
- She liked working/playing with… (without mentioning that it was that particular job that afforded her the fun)

Acceptable answer
- She could do homework/study <u>while they were asleep/in bed/after she put them to bed</u>

Unacceptable
- She could work <u>at the same time</u>

   b) What did she not like about her other job?   **2 points**

Acceptable answer
- The restaurant job was (very/too/quite) tiring/made her tired

Unacceptable answer
- (Nothing mentioned here)

Acceptable answer
- You had to smile all the time/always

Unacceptable answer
- You had to be friendly/happy/pleasant/nice
- You had to smile (on its own)

4)
   a) Why were her customers in a good mood?   **1 point**

Acceptable answer
   – *They were out for a good time/having fun/to relax*
   OR
   They were with their family <u>and/or</u> friends

NB Either verb or both groups of people

Unacceptable answer
   – *They were out for a meal*
   OR
   They know <u>her</u> family
   The restaurant was good fun for family and friends

  b) How did she benefit from this?   **1 point**

Acceptable answer
   – *They left <u>good/a lot of/more</u> tips*

Unacceptable answer
   – *They bought her drinks (mistranslation of pourboire)*
   – *she got tips (no mention of quantity/quality)*
   – *she got money from them (too vague)*

5) Why did Francine and her fellow workers get on well together?   **2 points**

Acceptable answer
   – *They were the same/similar age(s)*

Unacceptable answer
   – *They kept in contact/became good friends*

Acceptable answer
   – *They were working/were there for the same/similar reasons*

Unacceptable
   – *(Nothing mentioned here)*

6) What aspects of her job did Francine find difficult?   **2 points**

Acceptable answer
   – *It was difficult to <u>motivate herself/be/stay motivated</u> after a (long) day*
    <u>studying/at school</u>

Unacceptable answer
   – *She was working*
   – *...after a long <u>journey</u>*

Acceptable answer
   – *Childminding/baby-sitting/working with children/looking after children*
    brings a lot of responsibilities/demands a lot of care/attention

NB Must link childminding to responsibility

Unacceptable answer
– Children demand a lot of care/attention (no reference to her particular job requirements)

7)

a) What concern did her parents have about Francine's jobs? **1 point**

Acceptable answer
– They thought her studies/schoolwork might suffer/she wouldn't have time to study/her studies should come first
School work/grades are/were suffering (at least, that was their worry)
Parents are worried about her schoolwork/grades/worried that she is not studying

NB Must express key idea of general schoolwork/performance

Unacceptable answer
– She needs to study for her <u>exams</u> (too specific)
Parents are worried about her exams (also too vague – does not imply a link with her job)
Any implication of paid work (rather than schoolwork)

b) What did Francine do to meet this concern? [A difficult question to understand!] **2 points**

Acceptable
– She did extra/supplementary studying/work/schoolwork/at the weekends

Unacceptable answer
– She didn't work at the weekends
Any implication of doing (extra) paid work
She saves weekends for schoolwork
– She studied hard at weekends

Acceptable answer
– She stopped working/gave up her job/did not work (in the restaurant) when her exams were getting near/approaching/in the run-up to the exams/before her exams/when the exams were close
She stopped working until her exams were over
She worked until her exams were close

Unacceptable answer
– She cuts back on hours/tries not to work so much…
when she has exams/during/the night before her exams

She stopped working until her exams were close/at the time of her exams

8) According to Francine, how has she benefited from her jobs?   **2 points**

Acceptable answer
  – *Brought her happiness/made her happy*
  OR
  She <u>realised</u> there are more important things than (making) money

Unacceptable answer
  – *She was in a good mood/humour (mishearing of <u>bonheur</u>)*

Acceptable answer
  – *She (still) sees the children (every day/always)*
  OR
  Children (will/do) remember her/think of her

Unacceptable answer
  – *The children are adorable*
  She loved working with adorable children

The main point to be drawn from this marking scheme (and indeed all the others to date) is the emphasis on the need to explain your full understanding and to back this up by providing specific details.

Dos

✔ *Read through the introduction and questions in English carefully, as these form a kind of summary of the passage.*

✔ *Make sure the period before the actual first recording is used productively – you could imagine some logical answers at this stage!*

✔ *Use the 2 minute air time between playings to write down possible answers.*

✔ *Make sure that your handwriting is clear.*

 The Examiners' Report regularly makes reference to poor handwriting!

✔ *Concentrate on the general points of comprehension first – try to build an image of the situation as a foundation.*

✔ *Ensure you express the key idea each time.*

✔ Make all answers specific.

✔ Explain how you have arrived at these answers.

✔ Write down in French any key words you do not fully understand, so that these can be checked in the dictionary after the second playing (this assumes that you have practised pronunciation and spelling during the course).

✔ Jot down notes or abbreviations which you can later exemplify.

✔ Ensure that all aspects of the question are covered in your answers.

✔ Be explicit – leave nothing as implied.

✔ Include rather than exclude (you only lose marks for giving more than what is in the passage if it contradicts or negates the correct answer or is wildly wrong).

✔ Read through all your answers in order to check over your English.

Don'ts

✗ Allow a failure to answer one question affect your understanding of the whole page or the other questions.

✗ Leave blanks (you should be able to see how the marking instructions accept many variations of the correct answer, so something, even if it is clumsy or incomplete, stands you a better chance of picking marks.)

✗ Be content to give vague answers (even if these are right, they will be deemed insufficient.)

✗ Give answers which are too short and do not demonstrate full understanding of the text nor fully answer the question (very few questions are merely asking you to translate a single item of vocabulary.)

✗ (over-)interpret: stick to explaining just what is in the text, rather than adding anything to the original.

✗ Simply transcribe the text or write down all that you hear – stick to the tasks and answer the questions!

Some additional useful tips

Each time you practise with a listening exercise or do a past paper try to *get as much out of the passage* as you can. Consider some of these tips:

● Read through the passage first to give a little general support.

● Then make a note of some of the more difficult vocabulary or phrases.

● Go over the use of tenses – can you follow the switches from past to present to future?

- Check the points of view – whose opinion is being expressed at any one time?
- Do it as a listening exam, without the transcripts.
- Read over the transcript again – try a short part of the text as a translation exercise.

Build *variety* into your listening practice. Try out these types of comprehension skills at various points in your revision:

- General gist – list the main themes or ideas in the passage.
- Do a brainstorm sheet on what you hear – use diagrams, flow charts, any of the techniques for learning or revising that you learn in study skills lessons!
- Do a summary in English.
- Choose to concentrate on one particular perspective or part of the text.
- Pick a *type* of language, and extract the relevant details – e.g. descriptive language: write down all positive and negative adjectives in English or in French.
- Make a list of all verbs.
- Make three columns – PAST   PRESENT   FUTURE – and note the number of references to each.

Student activity

Create a tense grid, based on the actual transcript of the practice past paper you've been doing. Divide the grid into three sections: PAST – PRESENT – FUTURE, and jot down six examples (where possible). This will focus your attention on the all-important tense shifting that goes on in listening exams. Take the specimen paper as an example:

Past	Present	Future
Quelles matières as-tu étudiées?	Un prof qui n'aime pas ses élèves…	-
C'était très général	…qui n'aide pas…	-
Je ne voulais pas y aller	…qui crie beaucoup…	-
Le reste du lycée pensait que…	…qui fait des commentaires…	-
Tu as dit que tu as fait…	-	-
Comment as-tu trouvé les profs?	-	-

Of course, there may well be blanks; that is to say, that there may be nothing said (as in this case) in the future!

The key thing to note here is that you must use any revision or practice session to try out or learn something *new,* rather than just consolidate what you already know.

Finally, here is a short list of listening resources that you might find useful:

- Leckie and Leckie's *Higher French Course Notes* (again!) is helpful in so is many ways. Firstly, it breaks down into shorter texts the kind of language you will find in the longer exam passages; secondly, it provides a full transcript; thirdly, the answer booklet is easy to use. The fact that these passages are divided up into the three themes allows you to feel that you are building up knowledge and skills simultaneously.

- Use the Leckie and Leckie *Past Papers* which contain the full set of listening examinations, with an answer booklet at the back. This becomes an even more useful resource when used in conjunction with the actual MP3 recordings on the SQA website.

- Mary Glasgow Publications: the more advanced magazines have excellent listening exercises. While these may prove occasionally a little tricky to tie in with the reading passages, there is always a full transcript and the actual quality of recording and standard (and variety!) of listening texts is excellent.

- Use the Internet, especially the Learning Teaching Scotland website (type in Higher French listening resources and download the MP3 files – these are excellent activities, and can be used without a task or even questions).

- Still on the Internet, you should access the Leckie and Leckie past listening papers (2003–2008), which can be downloaded as MP3 files. The quality of sound is excellent.

5 | Written Response/ Short Essay

Part 1: General

Part 2: Specific

PART 1: GENERAL

The second part of paper II, section B, is writing. Here, you are issued with a statement about the listening passage you have just heard and then given a title in French in the form of a question, with the instruction, in French, to write your answer in 120–150 words. This piece of writing takes approximately 40 minutes, and is worth 10 marks (so 10% of the total). The same criteria and pegged points system are used to mark this as were used with the directed writing in paper I.

It is worth remembering that the directed writing (paper I) and the writing (paper II) together add up to 25% of the Higher examination.

So how does this task differ from the directed writing task, and what exactly are they testing here? The most obvious difference is that this is a personal response, rather than a prescribed task or set of instructions.

This is also a discursive piece of writing, involving both the structure and the presentation of points of view or argument. Like a traditional essay, this part of the examination invites you to back up thoughts and opinions on an issue by referring to your own experiences and those of others.

As with the other parts of the examination at Higher level there is plenty of preparation that can be done. Don't be fooled by the fact that some people refer to this section as the 'personal response' essay; while it is true that you certainly need to read and respond to the stimulus of the complicated-looking title, you are also expected *'to incorporate and adapt learned material which is relevant to the aspects contained in the stimulus'* (Examiners' Report on paper II, section B, writing, 2008 Higher French).

This is definitely an invitation to write out a number of paragraphs or even essays in *quality* French and commit them to memory, so that you can access this learned material in the examination.

PART 2: SPECIFIC

Much of what you have read about in this book on how to revise and prepare for the oral assessment and the directed writing can be applied to the short essay. The experiences of folio writings at Standard Grade and the writing examination of Intermediate 2 are useful background too, as they emphasise the need to be analytical about what goes into good written French.

Throughout your course, your teacher will encourage you to write essays on the major themes and topics. These will involve this same process of ensuring that you include the key vocabulary, a range of tenses, and descriptive, discursive language at a highly accurate level, in an organised and persuasive manner.

SQA examiners are constantly reminding schools that pupils should practise the kind of writing required in the (optional) Personal Record of Achievement, as it was designed to help candidates '*develop grammatical accuracy in handling present, past and future tenses and to focus on the accuracy that is required in terms of spelling, genders, accents and agreements*' (Examiners' Report, same source as above). The more you practise this kind of writing, the more likely it will be that your written papers in the exam contain all the essential features.

Before we proceed to focus on examples of the types of French you should incorporate into your short essay, let us have a quick reminder of the grade A features of writing, as laid out in the Arrangements Documents.

GRADE A (very good)
Content
• Information is presented in a *clear and structured way*.   • Writing *expresses and develops point of view* with a sense of structure.
Writing
• Shows good awareness of the *rules of grammar*, with few major errors.   • Uses more *complex sentences*, including a *range of structure* (or grammar) and *vocabulary/phrases*, and makes appropriate use of *memorised material*.

The first area to concentrate on is that of **_structure_**. This is important because the essay needs to respond to and deal with *all aspects of the title* (which, again, can appear a little over-complicated!) and, at the same time, *follow a line of* *argument* or at least a sense of development throughout. Of course, you will probably not be able to see a clear structure to the essay straight off, so a short period of *brainstorming*, or jotting down of ideas, is often needed before a real shape emerges. So here is a little reminder of the preparation steps:

Structure

Title

- Plan your essay to deal with the two or three major aspects in the title, and ensure that you refer to all the minor ones, by examining closely the details of the questions in French.

Brainstorm

- Jot down ideas under the separate headings or aspects of the title (including areas where you can call on learned material).
- Then prioritise these (dividing into main points and examples).
- Consider which other topics/memorised language you can bring to enrich your essay and broaden your essay.

Organisation

- Introduce your essay by referring to the main points in the title.
- Paragraphs are the best way to approach the main areas of discussion efficiently and convince the marker that you have reflected on and ordered your argument(s). (A tried and tested technique is to take the pros versus cons approach, as is the approach of taking each of the separate aspects of the main issue in turn.)
- Conclude with a reference to the full title, but do not repeat the introduction!

This is a useful time to reflect on the titles since 2001. A clear pattern emerges:

2001
Isabelle nous dit que les dangers du tabac ne l'inquiètent pas beaucoup.

Et vous? Vous pensez qu'il est important de penser à la santé?
Qu'est-ce que vous faites pour vous maintenir en forme?

2002
Adèle était contente d'aller à l'université à Montpellier après avoir quitté l'école.

Et vous, avez-vous un endroit préféré où vous aimeriez habiter?
Comptez-vous rester chez vous ou aller vivre ailleurs? Pour quelles raisons?

2003
Tristan apprécie la liberté qu'il a en vacances chez ses grands-parents.

Et vous? Est-ce que vous avez assez de liberté dans la vie?
Trouvez-vous que les adultes imposent trop de règles – à la maison, au collège ou en vacances, par exemple?

2004

Marie-Claire parle de ses plans pour l'avenir.

Et vous, quels sont vos plans pour une carrière?
A votre avis, est-ce qu'il est important de parler une langue étrangère?

2005

Annick nous parle du sport.

Est-ce qu'il y a assez de possibilités sportives là où vous habitez?
Est-ce que le sport est important pour vous?
A votre avis est-ce que les jeunes devraient faire plus de sport?

2006

Madame Fourniret nous parle de son collège.

A votre avis, quels sont les aspects importants d'un bon collège?
Voulez-vous continuer vos études après le collège ou entrer directement dans le monde du travail?

2007

Aurélie nous parle de sa vie dans une grande ville.

A votre avis, quels sont les avantages et les inconvénients d'habiter dans une grande ville?
Avez-vous l'intention de quitter votre ville pour suivre votre carrière?

2008

Les jobs de Francine lui ont apporté de l'argent.

Est-ce que vous avez assez d'argent pour vos besoins?
A votre avis, quels sont les avantages et les inconvénients d'avoir un emploi de temps partiel?

 The Short Essay is definitely one you should be well prepared for, and the essay topics have been quite limited to date. Best practice would be to write an essay in response to each of the past papers, using advice previously given in this book.

Student activity

The questions in the short essay invariably use the 'vous' form, and can be awkward to understand when you are under pressure. It is a useful (if tedious) exercise to copy out the questions and ensure that you understand them. You will discover that you can very soon grow more accustomed to phrases such as *Que pensez-vous de...?* and *Trouvez-vous que...?*

In each of the past papers, the passage is summarised first, before the two or three questions – each dealing with a different aspect of the topic – are posed. Taking the example of the **specimen paper** (which you can refer to via the SQA website) you could begin by brainstorming your ideas, without any fixed plan in mind:

What I want to do later?
Well paid job?
>Good grades in French/Spanish, so doing them!
>English & maths - no choice!

>parents   Guidance/Careers advice

>Mr Campbell, great teacher!

But then you can quickly order these ideas, according to the two aspects/ questions in the title, and perhaps even apply *positive* and *negative* points to give it more shape and balance. You will find that, at this stage, you will develop your better ideas and drop the weaker ones.

Influences

- *Have enjoyed French & Spanish (also French exchange/holidays in Spain)*
- *Great Biology teacher, encouraged me*
- *Hate maths, but have to!*
- *Mum forced me to do English (hate reading)*

Future

- *Would like to live/work abroad (weather/lifestyle)*
- *Brother spent 1 year in France & loved it!*
- *Couldn't work in office or with computers*
- *Tho' Biology good, don't fancy lab job*

You've spent only 3 minutes, but the structure has emerged clearly! Now, don't forget what's being tested and graded – it's the *quality of your written French* – so jot down a few important reminders/ideas of what to include:

Influences

- *Have enjoyed French & Spanish (also French exchange/holidays in Spain) [on a passé une quinzaine/il y a deux ans/vacances d'été]*
- *Great Biology teacher, encouraged me [mon prof de sciences nats m'a encouragé(e) je le trouvais très compréhensif]*
- *Hate maths, but have to! [il a fallu que je prenne]*
- *Mum forced me to do English (hate reading) [m'a obligé(e) de... /depuis l'âge de... + present]*

Future

- *Would like to live/work abroad (weather/lifestyle) [j'aimerais passer... /à cause du temps/mode de vie]*
- *Brother spent 1 year in France & loved it! [il l'a beaucoup apprécié]*
- *Couldn't work in office or with computers [je ne pourrais jamais... /ça ne me dirait rien de...]*
- *Tho' Biology good, don't fancy lab job [??]*

You're now almost 10 minutes into this section of the paper, but you are actually *ready to write*, having thought of ideas and a structure, and some of the tenses (present/perfect/imperfect/conditional/subjunctive) and high impact phrases (*il y a/obligé de... /ça ne me dirait rien de... /à cause du temps*). You've also dropped the idea of writing about not working in a laboratory, because you're not sure how to say it. Good decision! ***Don't write what you don't know!*** Your Higher French writing examination is definitely **NOT** the time to be experimenting!

OK, 30 minutes to go, and a very good mark to get... start writing for real.

(Reminder: underlinings refer to errors)

Je vais passer mes examens de Higher à la fin de l'année scolaire en français et espagnol, en biologie, anglais et (bien sûr) en maths.

Tout d'abord, j'ai toujours adoré les langues étrangères. Il y a deux ans, quand j'<u>etais</u> en troisième, j'ai passé une quinzaine en France avec notre échange scolaire. Quelle bonne expérience! En plus, nous allons presque tous les ans en <u>Espange</u> pour les vacances d'été, et c'est absolument formidable! Il fait beau et chaud <u>la'bas</u> et on s'amuse beaucoup. Mon père sait parler espagnol.

Il faut dire que j'aime aussi la biologie, car mon prof m'a encouragé de continuer avec ça. L'année dernière il était très compréhensif.

Je déteste les maths, mais il a fallu que je prenne ce sujet, c'est obligatoire. Et ma mère m'a obligé de prendre l'<u>anglias.</u>

A l'avenir, j'aimerais vivre en France ou en <u>Espange</u> – je ne sais pas <u>quel,</u> mais à l'<u>etranger.</u> Et pourquoi? Eh bien, à cause du temps et la façon de vivre! Je voudrais <u>peut etre</u> travailler à Paris <u>où</u> à Barcelone. Mais je ne pourrais jamais travailler avec les <u>ordinatuers,</u> j'ai horreur de ça! La technologie, ça ne me dit rien!

(211 words)

With 5 minutes to go, you do have time to *improve on this*. (Using the phrase 'checking over' simply has pupils nodding in agreement with what they've written.) What advice would *you* give here? You might want to consider, for example, using the dictionary to pick up on what could be a few costly errors:

- *Espange (x 2!)*
- *ordinatuers*
- *anglias*
- *la'bas*

These simple spelling mistakes really spoil the look of the essay and, because they are so basic, detract from the excellent French elsewhere. Then there is the issue of accents, which lose hundreds of candidates an A grade every year. So are they spelling errors, or worse? Look for yourself:

- *j'etais*
- *l'etranger*
- *(à Paris) où à Barcelone*
- *peut etre*

The answer to your question is, of course, to be found in the dictionary: you can't find *etais* (which should be *étais*) because it's the imperfect of the verb *être,* and you know the only part of the verb you can be sure of finding in the dictionary is the infinitive; *étranger* is the word, with the é, and *où* with the accent means *where,* but *ou* without is the one you want, meaning *or*; peut-être should be there in the dictionary, but there is a difference between the peut être as two words and as the single hyphenated one. Yes, the French language is sent to *test* us.

So, does this essay score a very good, or not? You should be able to provide an answer of your own, with reasons. With the corrections, my feeling is *yes*. The accuracy and range of the tense work are real strengths, and the turn of phrase is impressive, as is the clearly memorised material. The structure is fine; perhaps a little too much time has been spent on the first question, but on the whole there is a good response to both aspects of the title. As for the essay with all of the errors still in place, there might be doubt cast on the student's ability to control the language. The essay is introduced efficiently, and the paragraphs are broadly successful in dealing with the major points by quoting personal examples, and opinions and reasons are nicely combined. One of the problems here is the number of mistakes towards the end, which is very common, and this gives the sense of slackness in the French. Remember, accuracy is the most important feature, and despite the very good range of grammar and expression, you could do with fewer errors. Overall, I would still award this a very good as it convinces me with the following areas of success:

Tense work

- **good range: present/perfect/imperfect/future/conditional/subjunctive examples:**

  nous allons/il fait beau/mon père sait parler…/je déteste/ça ne me dit rien/je ne sais pas
  j'ai toujours adoré/j'ai passé/[il] m'a encouragé/[elle] m'a obligé de prendre…
  il était
  je vais passer
  j'aimerais vivre/je voudrais […] travailler/je ne pourrais jamais travailler
  il a fallu que je prenne

Expressions

- **some nice turns of phrase, giving the essay a French 'feel' examples:**

  bien sûr
  quelle bonne expérience!
  absolument formidable
  il faut dire que…
  et pourquoi?
  j'ai horreur de ça
  ça ne me dit rien!

- **and there is some smart use of time phrases, too examples:**

  à la fin de l'année scolaire
  il y a deux ans
  presque tous les ans
  pour les vacances d'été
  l'année dernière
  à l'avenir
  jamais

In addition to these strengths, the essay as a whole is convincingly accurate – the marker would be left in little doubt that the candidate had, in general, demonstrated proper control in his/her writing.

We have marked out what aspects of the structure are necessary for the short essay, and shown through the example above how that structure gives support and focus to the writing. Next, we should examine the range of tenses (as indeed we have done already in the chapters on oral assessment and directed writing). How could the specimen paper essay have been improved in respect of the variety of tense work? Here is a general approach you will find useful, whereby the candidate ensures that past, present and future tenses all feature convincingly in the essay:

Past

pluperfect

Quand j'étais en sixième, **j'avais aimé** les maths, mais l'année dernière j'ai détesté cette matière. (When I was in S1, I had liked maths, but last year I hated this subject.)

Mon père **était allé** en Espagne lorsqu'il était tout petit. (My father had been to Spain when he was small.)

- Note how the perfect j'*ai* aimé (I liked) becomes j'*avais* aimé (I had liked), by changing the auxiliary verb to the imperfect.

- See how the auxiliary is from *être* when using a verb which we know already takes *être* in the perfect tense – as when we use *aller, venir, sortir, rester, retourner*, etc. What is important is to remember that the past participle would 'agree' with the masculine/feminine and singular/plural (e.g. *elle était allée; ils étaient allés*, etc.).

Student activity

Since the pluperfect is a tense you will have used much less often than, say, the perfect, it makes sense to learn certain stock phrases off by heart that you can draw on when in the exam. Try forming six or so, some with *être* and others with *avoir*:

- quand j'étais plus jeune, j'étais allé(e) à l'étranger avec ma mere...
- je n'avais jamais aimé mon prof d'histoire...
  etc.

---

perfect

Mes amis ont tous laissé tomber les sciences, car ils les trouvaient extrêmement difficiles. (My friends all dropped the science subjects, as they found them extremely difficult.)

Je me suis décidé à prendre les langues vivantes…(I made up my mind to take modern languages…)

- Firstly, few candidates bother to discuss what others have done, so you have an ideal opportunity to do just that and use the third person plural in the perfect. Secondly, note how the *tous* shows off your ability to separate the subject (*mes amis*) from the verbs. Finally, this title of essay allows you to use the complicated *laissé tomber* – so it is always worthwhile storing a topic-specific high-impact structure such as this!

- Candidates avoid the reflexive verbs in the perfect like the plague – and no wonder. As a set phrase, however, it should be committed to memory *je me suis décidé(e) à* = I made up my mind to. Remember, a reflexive verb shows your understanding of the reflexive pronoun, the 'agreement' of the past participle with the subject (here: *je*), and definitely marks you out as a candidate aiming for a high grade.

imperfect

Mes parents n'étaient pas contents avec ma decision, mais ils devaient l'accepter. (My parents were not happy with my decision, but they had to accept it.)

Mon meilleur copain et moi, nous voulions absolument choisir la biologie…(My best friend and I absolutely wanted to take Biology…)

- The imperfect is a difficult tense to spell, as the endings contain some silent letters. However, it is a question of practice, as with spelling generally. The introduction of the negative shows that you know where the *ne* and *pas* fit with the imperfect (either side of the verb), and the extra verb proves that you understand what happens when you have two verbs, i.e. that it is the first of these that goes in the imperfect and the second in the infinitive.

- Students don't like the look of the nous *-ions* ending in the imperfect, and don't therefore use it enough to trust it in the exams. *Vouloir* is a verb that usually requires a second verb (again in the infinitive); to strengthen the expression the word *absolument* comes in between the two verbs.

Present

En choisissant mes matières pour cette année, j'ai décidé de...(In choosing my subjects for this year, I decided to...)

- The present participle is very underused! You don't have to include a subject pronoun with it and it looks the same whoever you are talking about!

Future

immediate future

J'espère continuer avec le français et je compte le perfectionner à l'étranger. (I hope to continue with French and intend to improve my language abroad.)

- This is such an easy tense to use, as the first verb is conjugated but the second stays in the infintive. (Try it with *je veux/peux/dois, j'ai l'intention de*, etc.)

real future

Je ferai peut-être une année sabbatique et j'irai en Afrique pour travailler avec les enfants. (Perhaps I'll do a gap year and go to Africa to work with children.)

- Again, these are rare, possibly because of their awkward look – but the irregulars (from *faire, aller*, etc.) are easily learned!

conditional (with two verbs)

Je devrais passer au moins six mois en France ou bien je pourrais aussi trouver du travail en Espagne. (I should spend at least six months in France or else I could also find work in Spain.)

- The first verb is in the conditional, the second in the infinitive; learning the equivalents of I should (*je devrais*), I could (*je pourrais*), I would like to (*je voudrais* or *j'aimerais*) and I would prefer to (*je préférerais*) is a real confidence booster as these can be used in just about any writing piece and are especially useful for the concluding paragraph!

imperfect with conditional

Si j'avais le temps, j'aimerais voyager en Amérique du Sud. (If I had the time, I would like to travel around South America.)
Si j'étais riche, je'achèterais une belle maison dans le Midi. (If I were rich, I would buy a nice house in the Midi.)

- Both follow the imperfect-followed-by-conditional rule; the second example uses a single verb only.

Subjunctive (a very limited approach!)

Even if you are unfamiliar with this tense, you can still learn a couple of the subjunctive phrases.

il faut que... (I have to...) in present/past/future:

> Il faut que je **prenne** les maths et l'anglais, car ils sont obligatoires. (I have to take maths and English, as they are obligatory subjects.)
> Il a fallu que je **prenne**...(I had to take...)
> Il va falloir que je **prenne**...(I will have to take...)
> Il faudra que je **prenne**...(I will have to take...)

● Note how the subjunctive *je prenne* is not required to change here according to the tense at the start of the sentence!

bien que/quoique...(although...) in present tense only:

> Bien que ce soit important, l'anglais ne m'intéresse pas du tout! (Although it is important, English doesn't interest me at all!)
> Quoique ce soit difficile, l'espagnol est intéressant. (Although it is difficult, Spanish is interesting.)

● The subjunctive is basically a mood tense, or one which is used after a number of expressions/conjunctions, and this is not the place to teach it. However, squeezing a sentence with *il faut que*...(in whatever tense) or *bien que/quoique*...into your short essay creates a positive impression.

Student activity

Now that you have been taken through this essay and shown its good (and less good) features, you ought to try your own essay on this topic.

Finally, I promised that we would have a look at how the use of discursive and time phrases would add significantly to the overall quality of your written French. Let us look at how this particular essay could, for example, have benefited from some of these, while bearing in mind how these expressions could be transferred to writing about other topics.

Introduction (to the essay or a particular point)	
Tout d'abord, examinons le système scolaire...	First of all, let us examine the school system...
Premièrement, je n'avais pas envie de faire les maths...	Firstly, I did not want to do maths...
Pour commencer, mon professeur m'a découragé de prendre le dessin...	For a start, my teacher discouraged me from taking art...
(add your own)	

Conclusion (of the essay or a particular point)	
Finalement, j'étais persuadé de continuer avec le latin.	In the end, I was persuaded to carry on with Latin.
Toute réflexion faite, c'était pour moi la bonne décision.	On reflection, it was the right decision for me.
Après avoir réfléchi, j'ai accepté de faire la physique.	Having thought about it, I agreed to do physics.
(add your own)	

Time phrases	
Past	
Il y a deux ans, j'ai passé mes examens de Standard Grade. (L'équivalent du Brevet en France.)	Two years ago, I sat my Standard Grades. (The equivalent of the Brevet in France.)
Au commencement, j'ai trouvé le prof un peu sévère.	At the beginning, I found the teacher a bit strict.
Au fur et à mesure de l'année scolaire, j'ai vraiment perfectionné mon français.	As the year at school progressed, I really improved my French.
(add your own)	
Present	
Cette année, je suis stressé(e) à cause du programme chargé.	This year, I'm stressed on account of the workload.
Maintenant, j'ai une vie scolaire plus équilibrée.	Now, I have a more balanced school life.
Actuellement, j'ai trop de devoirs.	At present, I have too much homework.
(add your own)	

Future	
Dans dix ans, je travaillerai en France peut-être.	In ten years' time, I'll be working in France perhaps.
A l'avenir, j'aimerais trouver la femme de mes rêves et avoir trois enfants.	In the future I would like to find the woman of my dreams and have three children.
Quand j'aurai vingt ans, je quitterai la faculté.	When I am twenty, I will leave university.
(add your own)	

A very good short essay is likely to contain the types of language features which we have looked at in the sections on structure, range of tenses and phrases. A satisfactory essay will probably have fewer of the essential features, with less range and accuracy. Examples of both of these levels of writing in relation to the 2008 paper should offer an insight into the crucial differences between a satisfactory (6/10) and a very good (10/10) essay.

2008
Les jobs de Francine lui ont apporté de l'argent.

Est-ce que vous avez assez d'argent pour vos besoins?
A votre avis, quels sont les avantages et les inconvénients d'avoir un emploi à temps partiel?

Ecrivez 120–150 mots en français pour exprimer vos idées.

Satisfactory

Toutes les semaines mes parents <u>donnent</u> de l'argent de poche. Donc, je peux acheter des CDs le week-end et sortir le samedi soir. Mais <u>c'est</u> ne pas assez parce que je ne peux pas <u>achter</u> mes v<u>é</u>tements préférés – c'est trop cher! (43)

Je voudrais avoir un temps partiel comme Francine – du babysitting ou travailler dans un supermarché. Ma mère dit NON, tu dois faire les devoirs! C'est pénible! Ce n'est pas juste. Mon <u>ami</u> Carole travaille tous les soirs chez Top Man et elle <u>acheté</u> une voiture. Carole est intelligente <u>at</u> bavarde avec les cheveux blonds. Elle est très mince. (59)

Dans le futur je voudrais gagner <u>beacoup de</u> argent et habiter dans une grande maison en France. J'<u>aime</u> deux voitures – une Porsche et une ferari! Mais c'est nécessaire d'avoir de l'argent! (34)

(136 words)

Analysis

You should jot down a couple of points of your own before reading my ideas!

The structure is just about adequate in that the candidate deals with most of what is in the title in a recognisable fashion: she addresses both the idea of not having enough money for her (limited) needs and implies that her friend is able to buy a car with what she earns in her part-time job. However, there is no formal introduction or conclusion and links are not explicit. Nor is there an attempt to write systematically about the pros and cons of having a job. There is also some irrelevant material, such as the description of Carole.

The accuracy is satisfactory in so far as the majority of the tense endings are correct, and there is some range from past to present (*je peux acheter*; *ma mère dit NON*; *mon ami Carole travaille*, etc.) to future (*je voudrais avoir*; *je voudrais gagner*). But there are problems here, too: the object is missed out of the opening sentence (*mes parents me donnent de l'argent* is what we are looking for), and *ce n'est pas juste* is the correct form. Also, the one example of the perfect is botched, as the correct auxiliary verb in *elle a acheté* is missing. The grasp of the future is undermined by the use of the present instead, in *j'aime deux voitures*.

Having said that, the overall spelling is sound enough, though slack (missing accents don't help, and beaucoup really isn't that hard). And there is certainly a decent attempt at phrases and expressions (*donc*; *mais*; *c'est pénible*; *c'est nécessaire de…*), although the question is whether this candidate is operating at Higher or sub-Higher level. I conclude that he/she is – just!

6/10

Very good

Tout d'abord, à mon avis il est <u>absoluement</u> nécessaire de trouver un job à temps partiel comme Francine. Mes parents n'ont pas assez d'argent pour m'acheter tout ce qu'il faut et par <u>consequent</u> je dois gagner de l'argent au supermarché. Je travaille deux soirs par semaine au supermarché et je gagne environ trente livres par semaine – ça me permet d'acheter ce que je veux. Par exemple, la semaine dernière, je suis allé en ville avec mes amis et nous avons mangé au Quick et après nous avons vu un bon film d'horreur au cinéma et j'ai tout payé! Mes parents étaient reconnaissants!

Mais, de l'autre côté, il y a beaucoup d'inconvénients aussi d'avoir un emploi à mon âge: premièrement, c'est fatigant. Hier, après avoir travaillé trois heures au supermarché j'ai dû faire mes devoirs de maths et j'étais crevé!

En plus, si on gagne de l'argent, on a pas le temps pour se détendre. J'aimerais jouer au golf avec mon père, mais je suis occupé. C'est dommage parce que je suis très sportif!

En conclusion, je dirais qu'il y a des avantages et des inconvénients de gagner sa vie quand vous êtes au lycée. Il faut que la vie soit équilibrée!

(209 words)

Analysis

As with the satisfactory essay, I would urge you to try to analyse some of the strengths and weaknesses before starting to read my own analysis.

The structure of this essay is appropriately formal for an examination, introducing the general and specific issues in turn before concluding. There is a nice balance between the candidate's own experiences and examples and the broader aspects of the title.

The quality of language is the most outstanding feature, however. The candidate is determined to show that he is competent in both present and perfect tenses: there are several examples of using two verbs together (*mes parents n'ont pas assez d'argent pour m'acheter…; je dois gagner…; ça me permet d'acheter…*) and the number of accurate perfects at the end of the opening paragraph is impressive (*je suis allée; nous avons mangé; nous avons vu; j'ai tout payé*) before giving us the difficult *j'ai dû faire mes devoirs* in the second paragraph.

There are only a couple of future conditionals (*j'aimerais jouer au golf; je dirais que…*) but they are entirely appropriate. The subjunctive at the end seems a little rehearsed (*il faut que la vie soit équilibrée*), but that is not a disadvantage!

The descriptive language is also strong: his parents were *reconnaissants* (grateful); the job is *fatigant* (tiring), he admits to being *crevé* (exhausted); life needs to be *équilibrée* (balanced).

The sentence structure is varied, with a number of complex sentences giving extra detail of exemplification.

There are many other positive aspects of the French, such as the 'argument' turns of phrase: *tout d'abord; à mon avis; par conséquent; par exemple; de l'autre côté; en plus; en conclusion*. But the little extras, such as *absolument nécessaire, c'est dommage, je dirais que* also add richness and idiom to the essay.

The title is dealt with fully in controlled, advanced and accurate language.

10/10

Dos

✔ *Include relevant memorised material.*

✔ *Plan your approach to the essay, covering all aspects of the title and create some links with other topics if this allows you to use more variety of language.*

✔ *Include in your plan some language items, especially tense work (past/ present/future).*

✔ *Ensure you divide up the essay into paragraphs.*

✔ *Make explicit links between your examples and the general points of argument (by giving examples, opinions followed by reasons).*

✔ *Include descriptive language.*

✔ *Include some advanced vocabulary – make sure that you clearly are writing at Higher level!*

✔ *Check over your work thoroughly.*

Don'ts

✗ *Go straight into writing without planning.*

✗ *Fail to introduce the general point before giving opinions or examples.*

✗ *Force the marker to make links between your examples and the main points for himself/herself.*

✗ *Regurgitate learned material which has no relevance.*

✗ *Write sentences without thinking about their quality – remember that the level of language is always more important than the point you are trying to make.*

✗ *Translate word for word from the English.*

✗ *Over-complicate your ideas or sentences.*

✗ *Go too far the required word count – unless you are highly confident of the level of accuracy.*

Points to remember

✔ By far the most useful resource for quality essay-type French is Leckie and Leckie's *Higher French Course Notes*, where there is an excellent chapter on sentences and phrases across all the major topics, Test Yourself (pages 89–92).

✔ Of course, testing yourself is something that you can do only after you have tried to learn the material first. If there is one thing I hope to have conveyed to you, it is that so much in the French Higher examinations depends on how well you have really learned the basic course material. Especially in the oral and writing parts, preparation is the key – and memorising white understanding leads to success!

✔ Do your very best – a top grade, whether A or B, is achievable by most students who put in the effort! Many a candidate will achieve such a grade at French Higher who may not consider himself/herself to be a particularly gifted linguist!